VANGUARD SERIES

EDITOR: MARTIN WINDROW

THE STUART LIGHT TANK SERIES

Text by BRYAN PERRETT

Colour plates by DAVID E. SMITH

OSPREY PUBLISHING LONDON

Published in 1980 by
Osprey Publishing Ltd
Member company of the George Philip Group
12–14 Long Acre, London WC2E 9LP
© Copyright 1980 Osprey Publishing Ltd
Reprinted 1985

This book is copyrighted under the Berne Convention. All rights reserved. Apart from any fair dealing for the purpose of private study, research, criticism or review, as permitted under the Copyright Act, 1956, no part of this publication may be reproduced, stored in a retrieval system, or transmitted in any form or by any means, electronic, electrical, chemical, mechanical, optical, photocopying, recording or otherwise, without the prior permission of the copyright owner. Enquiries should be addressed to the Publishers.

ISBN 0 85045 370 4

Filmset in Great Britain
Printed in Hong Kong

Acknowledgements
The author would like to offer his thanks to Colonel Peter Hordern and Lieutenant-Colonel Kenneth Hill of the RAC Tank Museum for their invaluable advice on a number of technical points, in particular concerning the workings of the Combination Gun Mounts M20 and M22; and to Captain Harry Travis for his time spent in detailing alterations made to standard vehicles by 7th Light Cavalry in Burma. Thanks are also due to the US Army Military History Institute and to the Historical Section US Marine Corps for permitting access to their archives; to Steven Zaloga; and to Daniel Ambrogi for his advice and assistance over illustrations of Free French Stuarts.

Light Tank Development

In 1919, as part of the general disarmament programme following the First World War, the infant United States Tank Corps was disbanded as a separate arm of service. Contemporary opinions among General Staff officers paralleled those in other armies in considering that 'the primary mission of the tank is to facilitate the uninterrupted advance of the rifleman in the attack'; and this doctrine received official sanction in the 1920 National Defense Act which confirmed that tank training, tactics and development were the sole responsibility of the Chief of Infantry.

It was decided to follow the lead of the French in having two classes of tank for infantry support —a medium tank with which to lead the assault, and a light tank which would accompany the main body of the attack. The French Renault FT exercised a considerable influence on the views of what was required for the second class; and, conscious of its ability to be carried *portee* on the back of a lorry, thus saving valuable track mileage, in 1926 the Chief of Infantry requested the Ordnance Department to produce a two-man vehicle which was proof against small arms ammunition, was armed with a 37mm gun and which weighed not more than five tons.

In 1928 came the first signs that views were beginning to change. The establishment of the Experimental Mechanized Force in Great Britain had attracted a great deal of interest, and the US Army decided to set up its own Mechanized Force at Fort Eustis, Virginia. This consisted of mechanized elements of the three traditional arms, cavalry, infantry and artillery, supported by the new medium and light tanks as these became available.

A further advance was made when General Douglas MacArthur was appointed Army Chief of Staff in 1931. MacArthur was a strong advocate of mechanization who appreciated that to carry out its various rôles efficiently in the future the cavalry would have to be equipped with armoured vehicles, and when the Mechanized Force moved from Fort Eustis to Fort Knox, Kentucky, in 1932 it came under cavalry control. From that point the cavalry took the lead in

M1A1 Combat Car command vehicle used by Maj.-Gen. George S. Patton, commanding 2nd Armored Division, during 3rd Army's 1941 Louisiana Manoeuvres. The colour scheme is illustrated in Vanguard 11, *US 2nd Armored Division*, Plate A1. (US National Archives)

fighting vehicle development (although its tanks were called Combat Cars to circumvent the complexities of the National Defense Act), and the establishment of the 7th Cavalry Brigade (Mechanized) marked the birth of America's first truly armoured formation.

For the rest of the decade infantry and cavalry pursued their different philosophies until, on 10 July 1940, the War Department ordered the fusion of the two interests in the new Armored Force. At this time, when the German *blitzkrieg* had just swept across Europe, the United States possessed between 400 and 500 fighting vehicles of all types, of which all save a tiny handful of new medium and light tanks were completely obsolete by European standards.

The light tank series had its origins in the 1926 specification mentioned above. Because the Army as a whole was starved of funds it could only afford to produce one or two experimental designs each year and the first light tank prototypes, the T1 series, evolved slowly over the next four years and culminated in the **T1E4** of 1931, which established the standard American light tank layout of a rear-mounted engine and a forward drive sprocket.

The T1 series, with their low maximum speed of 12mph, did not fit in with MacArthur's ideas on mobility, and in 1933 the new **T2** was designed. This carried a crew of four and was armed with one .30 cal. machine gun in the front plate and a second mounted co-axially with a .50 cal. machine gun in the turret. The T2 weighed $7\frac{1}{2}$ tons and was powered by a 250hp air-cooled seven-cylinder Continental aero engine which produced a top speed of 35mph. The running gear consisted of two four-bogie units suspended from horizontal leaf-springs, front sprocket, rear idler and two return rollers, and was in fact copied from the Vickers Six-Tonner design.

Apparently the leaf-spring suspension did not stand up well to sustained high-speed running; it was replaced by vertical volute springing employed in conjunction with two two-wheel bogie units on a second prototype, the **T2E1**. This vehicle was similarly armed to the T2, but the turret was fixed and extended across the width of the hull. A further variation was the **T2E2** which carried twin limited-traverse turrets, one for each machine gun. The T2E1 and T2E2 were standardized respectively as **Light Tanks M2A1** and **M2A2**, and taken into service by the infantry.

The **T2E3** was very similar to the T2E1 but was equipped with a fully-rotating hand traversed turret. This vehicle had been designed for cavalry use and was standardized as **Combat Car M1**. An improved version, the **Combat Car M2**, had a rectangular turret, was powered by a Guiberson air-cooled radial diesel engine, and employed a trailing idler which increased ground contact and so provided more stable riding. Following the formation of the Armored Force, Combat Car M1 became **Light Tank M1A1** and Combat Car M2 **Light Tank M1A2**.

The **Light Tank M2A3** was essentially a refinement of the M2A2 incorporating a better

Light Tank M2A2 training with infantry, summer 1940. Note turret insignia: the brass crossed rifles of the infantry, on blue plaque, above the yellow/red/blue triangle of the Armored Force. (US National Archives)

transmission and thicker frontal armour. The performance of the suspension was improved by setting the bogie units further apart and employing longer vertical springs.

Thus far the M2 series had reflected the international fashion in arming light tanks with automatic weapons of various calibres. However, the **Light Tank M2A4**, which appeared in 1939, represented an important advance in that the vehicle's main armament was a 37mm M5 gun with an armour-piercing capability. This was mounted in a single riveted turret, co-axially with a .30 cal. machine gun, while further .30 cal. guns were located in the glacis plate and the two sponsons. If an anti-aircraft mounting was fitted this brought the number of automatic weapons available to five and this, together with the 37mm main armament, made the M2A4 one of the most formidably armed light tanks in the world. The Russian T-26B, which performed a similar rôle, and which could also claim descent from the Vickers Six-Tonner, was in fact armed with a 45mm gun and a co-axial machine gun, but could not match the American vehicle's cumulative firepower.

The M2A4 retained the hull and running gear of the M2A3, but was fitted with a synchromesh gearbox providing five forward and one reverse gear. An increase in the thickness of the frontal and side armour to 25mm brought the vehicle's weight up to 12 tons, which had the effect of reducing the top speed to 25mph.

Following the fall of France the US Army set about its massive re-armament programme, and immediate steps were taken to improve the M2A4 design in the light of the lessons provided by the German *blitzkrieg*. These resulted in the **Light Tank M3**, which had 37mm armour and thicker engine decks as a defence against air attack. This raised the overall weight to $13\frac{1}{2}$ tons, but this was absorbed by employing the trailing idler first used on the Combat Car M2, so that the vehicle was actually a little faster than the M2A4.

Early production turrets followed the octagonal pattern of the M2A4 and were also of

Light Tank M2A3 shows its paces to a class of reserve officers: note slightly wider spacing of bogie units. (US National Archives)

Interesting line-up of American armour at Fort Benning, Ga., April 1940. Left to right: the M2 Medium, from which the Lee was developed; the experimental T2 Medium; and the M2A3 Light. (US National Archives)

riveted construction, but shortly after the production run commenced riveting gave way to welding, as experience had shown that rivets were a serious danger to the crew when 'popped' by enemy fire. Later a cast turret of horseshoe section was introduced. The M2A4 turret had been well provided with ports, but the number of these was considerably reduced on the M3. From mid-1941 the main armament was fitted with a gyro-stabilizer.

Like its predecessors the M3 was powered by the Continental radial petrol engine. However, by 1942 the production of Continental engines had fallen behind that of M3 chassis, and the Guiberson radial diesel engine provided a reliable substitute. An unfortunate feature of the tank's design was the limited fuel capacity of 56 gallons which severely curtailed its operational radius; in view of the nature of the fighting in North Africa the British purchasing mission found this unacceptable and requested the additional provision of two 25-gallon jettison tanks. Sand shields were also fitted as standard on vehicles supplied to the British Army.

M3 production began in March 1941 and ended in August 1942, during which period 5,811 were built, including 1,285 diesel versions. In British service the vehicle was known as the 'General Stuart' in honour of the Civil War cavalryman, and also acquired the unofficial nickname of 'Honey' because of its pleasing handling characteristics and reliability; claims that this name was bestowed by a British tank driver are considered to be apocryphal—a more credible source is the American technical instruction team which accompanied the first consignment to the Middle East.

Further improvements to the basic design appeared in the **Light Tank M3A1**, which commenced production in April 1942, and which for a while was built concurrently with the M3. This was reflected by the last few M3s having a welded hull while the first M3A1s retained the riveted hull, before welding became standard. The major differences between the two vehicles were that the M3A1 dispensed with a cupola and was fitted with two turret hatches; the installation of an oil motor power traverse; and the provision of a turret basket, which the M3 had lacked. Minor modifications included the repositioning of the turret vision ports and, as the series progressed, the removal of the two sponson machine guns, the mountings for which were blanked off. The M3A1 was manufactured until February 1943, a total of 4,621 being built, of which 211 were diesel-powered.

Operational experience with the US Army and Marine Corps had confirmed not only the validity of the British criticism concerning low fuel capacity, but also that the M3's frontal armour was poorly arranged. The **Light Tank M3A3**, which entered production in December 1942, succeeded in remedying both faults. (M3A2 was to have been the designation of the welded M3A1 but was not adopted.)

This was done by extending the glacis plate upwards to meet the hull roof, thus eliminating the driver's and hull gunner's front hatches which were replaced by overhead hatches.

simultaneously, the sponsors were extended forwards to join the glacis by means of angled plates, the extra internal space being taken up by additional fuel tanks and general stowage. Following British practice, the radio was relocated in the turret, which was given a small overhang. In all 3,427 M3A3s were built before the M3 series was finally discontinued in August 1943; they served mainly in the armies of America's allies.

In the meantime, a second series of light tanks had been produced in parallel. This came about directly as a result of the 1941/42 shortage of Continental radial engines, which caused the Ordnance Department to seek an alternative power pack from the commercial motor vehicle industry. Cadillac suggested that two of their standard V-8 petrol engines working in tandem could supply the required output, and that this could be used in conjunction with their Hydra-

---

The Stuart Family Tree

Name in British Service

T1E4
Rear engine, front drive

T2
Continental radial engine

T2E1
Vertical volute springing
Single fixed turret
Light Tank M2A1

T2E3
Single traversable turret
Combat Car M1
Light Tank M1A1

T2E2
Twin turrets
Light Tank M2A2

Combat Car M2
Light Tank M1A2
Trailing idler
Guiberson radial engine

Light Tank M2A3

Light Tank M2A4
37mm main armament in
single traversable turret

Stuart

Light Tank M3
Continental engine
Guiberson engine

Stuart I
Stuart II

Light Tank M3A1
Continental engine
Guiberson engine

Stuart III
Stuart IV
Stuart V

Light Tank M3A3

Light Tank M3E2
Twin Cadillac engines
Light Tank M5
Light Tank M5A1

Stuart VI

T = vehicle under development   M = design standardized for production
A = major modification   E = experimental version

M2A4 Light Tanks of 66th Armored Regt., 2nd Armored Div. during the Louisiana Manoeuvres of 1941. (US National Archives)

matic automatic transmission. An M3 was made available for conversion, and the project designated **M3E2**. Its viability was demonstrated by a 500-mile test run which was entirely free from faults.

The automatic transmission occupied less internal space than the synchromesh system and a second experimental vehicle, the **M3E3**, showed that this made possible the installation of a better turret basket than that fitted to the M3A1. The M3E3 was standardized as the **Light Tank M5** in February 1942, and was manufactured by Cadillac and Massey-Harris. The hull of the M5 resembled that of the M3A3, but was easily distinguished by the stepped rear deck which was necessary for the accommodation of the two engines. An M3A1 turret was employed, complete with gyro-stabilizer.

In December 1942 the M3A3 turret became available and this represented such an improvement that it was at once fitted to the M5 chassis, the composite vehicle being designated **Light Tank M5A1**. Further modifications incorporated in this Mark included traverse facilities for the commander, an escape manhole in the hull floor, removable sand shields, and a stowage box fitted to the rear of the turret. The vehicle remained in production until June 1944 when the Army down-graded its status to substitute standard following the appearance of the M24, a light tank of modern design armed with a 75mm gun. Altogether, some 2,074 M5s and 6,810 M5A1s were built; the latter figure reflects the participation of the American Car and Foundry Company with Cadillac and Massey-Harris following the termination of the M3 series, for which they had been solely responsible.

Parallel Developments and Special-purpose Vehicles

A search for a more powerfully armed light tank with thicker armour had, in fact, begun in 1940 and resulted in the **Light Tank T7** series. These vehicles employed a version of the M3 suspension, later modified with horizontal as opposed to vertical volute springing. The early models were also powered by the Continental radial engine, but as the series progressed a variety of power packs and transmissions were tried, of which the Wright R-975 was preferred. The **T7E2**, which had a cast superstructure and turret and was armed with a 57mm gun, became the approved design, but was not standardized because the Armored Force had increased its basic requirements to a 75mm gun and a maximum armour thickness of 63mm. By the time these modifications had been incorporated the vehicle's weight had risen to 25 tons, taking it out of the light and into the medium tank class. The design was actually standardized as **Medium Tank M7**, but trials revealed an unsatisfactory power-to-weight ratio, and since the Medium M4 Sherman was already in quantity production it was abandoned after only seven vehicles had been built.

Another tank which employed a modified M3 suspension was the **Light Tank M22 (Airborne), Locust.** This weighed eight tons and was driven by a Lycoming 162hp petrol engine which produced a top speed of 40mph. The vehicle was armed with a 37mm gun and one .30 cal. machine gun, and had 25mm frontal armour. The crew consisted of commander, gunner and driver. Although 830 Locusts were built by Marmon-Herrington, who had also done the original design work, none was used operationally by the US Army, as a suitable transport aircraft

Light Tank M3 of the US Marine Corps with its full complement of machine guns; in this shot the gunner can just be seen squatting on the transmission housing between the driver and hull gunner. At 8ft 3in. the M3 was tall for its class. (US Marine Corps)

was not available; it was possible to sling the hull beneath the belly of a C-54 Skymaster transport while the turret travelled in the aircraft itself, but this method of shipment was obviously never intended for tactical employment.

The British, on the other hand, had developed the large Hamilcar glider to carry their own Tetrarch airborne tank, and they purchased a number of Locusts, which were of comparable weight and dimensions. In British service a Littlejohn adaptor was fitted to the 37mm, increasing the muzzle velocity by applying squeeze to the shot. A handful of these tanks accompanied the 6th Airlanding Brigade of the British 6th Airborne Division near the village of Hamminkeln during the Rhine crossings of 24 March 1945.

The M3/M5 chassis also provided the basis for a variety of experimental gun, howitzer and mortar motor carriages, but was too light and too narrow for favourable results to be achieved, and the majority of these projects were abandoned. A notable exception was the **75mm Howitzer Motor Carriage M8,** which employed an M5 chassis on which the short pack howitzer was mounted in a fully-rotating open-topped turret. As the turret had both front and rear overhangs which would have fouled the driver's and operator's hatches, it was necessary to relocate these in the glacis plate at the expense of the hull machine gun. The howitzer could be elevated to +40° and depressed to −20°. As only 46 rounds could be stowed inboard, the vehicle often towed a trailer containing a supplementary ammunition supply. The M8 was manufactured by Cadillac between September 1942 and January 1944, by which time 1,778 had been built. It served in the close-support rôle in reconnaissance units and the headquarters companies of medium tank battalions until eventually replaced by the M4A3 Medium Tank armed with a more powerful 105mm howitzer.

Both the M3 and M5 were fitted with various types of flame-throwing equipment. Of these the **Satan**, developed by the US Marine Corps for use against Japanese bunkers, was the most successful, a short projector replacing the 37mm main armament of an M3 or M3A1. The Canadian Ronson system was employed, giving

The M3A1 dispensed with the cupola, thus lowering the height to 7ft 6½in., and introduced hatches for both commander and gunner. This tank, serving with the British 8th Army in the desert, has been fitted with smoke-grenade dischargers; the sponson guns have been removed and an additional stowage locker has been welded in place on the left front, as viewed. (RAC Tank Museum)

(Right) The M3A3's armour was better arranged than on previous models, although the gun could now foul the driving compartment hatches. This tank belongs to the Chinese 1st Provisional Tank Unit, which served in northern Burma with a team of American advisors. (US Army Military History Institute)

a maximum range of 60 yards, and 170 gallons of flaming liquid was carried internally. The first 20 vehicles were converted in 1943, and subsequently a number of M5A1s were also fitted with the Satan equipment. If Satan conversions were not available for a particular operation the **E5R2 portable flame-thrower kit** could be used to give all Marks of the M3 and M5 series a flame capability, the projector simply replacing the hull machine gun. However, only 10 gallons of flaming liquid were supplied with the kit, and endurance was therefore very limited. Nonetheless, this equipment was widely used by the US Army and Marine Corps in the Pacific theatre of war.

A quadruple .50 cal. anti-aircraft mounting was tested experimentally on an M3 chassis, and a multiple rocket launcher was fired from the turret of an M5, but in the event both weapon systems found a more satisfactory carriage in other, larger, vehicles.

Turretless Stuarts were employed in a variety of rôles by both the British and American armies. The British used them as command vehicles with extra radios fitted, as Kangaroos (armoured personnel carriers), as armoured ambulances and as reconnaissance vehicles, generally with a folding canvas roof as a protection against bad weather. The Americans also had two command versions of their own, distinguished by a rectangular open-topped box built around the turret ring; the early models used an unaltered M3 chassis, but later vehicles employed what was in fact an M5 chassis with the hull converted to the M8 Howitzer Motor Carriage specification. The M5 chassis was also diverted to the reconnaissance rôle following the appearance of the Light Tank M24 in 1944.

The Stuart Described

Layout

The standard layout of the Stuart series remained unaltered throughout its history, and contained three basic elements: an engine compartment at the rear, a fighting compartment, and a driving

compartment. The fighting compartment housed the vehicle commander, who also acted as loader and subsequently as his own operator following the installation of the turret radio in the M3A3 and M5A1, and the gunner, who was placed on the left of the main armament. The propeller shaft passed through the fighting compartment to the gearbox and final drive unit, which ran across the front of the driving compartment to the sprockets. The driver was located on the left of the gearbox and the hull gunner/co-driver on the right; the co-driver was also radio operator on all Marks except the M3A3 and M5A1.

To anyone brought up in the relatively spacious confines of a modern main battle tank, the Stuart seems horribly cramped and dangerously overcrowded. However, those who served in the vehicle had no such yardstick to measure these things by, and accepted them as the norm. It was not, by any standards, a comfortable vehicle. When the 37mm or co-ax machine gun was in action the interior quickly filled with nauseating fumes. In cold weather the engine sucked freezing air through the fighting compartment; in tropical climates the turret crew could not remove their shirts without risking a burn from the hot metal.

Neither the M2A4 nor the M3 had a turret basket, which meant that the commander and gunner had to move round with the turret—something which the high propeller shaft casing made far from easy. Both of these models were fitted with a rudimentary cupola which was inconveniently situated to the left of their centre-line, and which, moreover, represented the *only* means of exit from the turret in an emergency.

This difficulty was resolved by the provision of commander's and gunner's hatches in the turret of the M3A1, but the fitting of a turret basket to the same Mark simply turned the vehicle into a killer. Because the propeller shaft inevitably took a high line from the centre of the radial engine, the floor of the basket was also high, and this could and frequently did block the escape route from the driving to the fighting compartment: the removal of a wounded man through the small aperture remaining was impossible without risking agony or further injury, even if time permitted. In Burma, the 7th Light Cavalry did not

The M5 employed the same turret as the M3A1, but the shape of the engine compartment had to be altered to accommodate the twin Cadillac engines. (RAC Tank Museum)

believe the risks were justified and had the turret baskets stripped out of their M3A1s, even though it meant that the turret crew had to stand and, if necessary, perch on the propeller shaft housing to look out of their hatches.

The twin propeller shafts of the M5 and M5A1's Cadillac engines naturally took a lower line and it was therefore possible to fit a deeper turret basket, thus disposing of the problem. However, a fresh difficulty arose in that the main armament generally fouled one or other of the overhead hatches with which the driving compartment of the M5 was fitted, and this could only be resolved by the installation of an escape manhole on the M5A1, as already described.

Automotive

Compared with the low, elegant British Crusader the Stuart was an ugly, sit-up-and-beg sort of vehicle, but it was a byword for reliability, rarely broke down, and refused to shed its tracks no matter how many tight, high-speed turns it was subjected to. It was also easy to maintain, and the radial engine could be removed quickly and easily simply by suspending a block and tackle from any convenient, stout branch.

The Continental engine was designed to run only on high-octane petrol, and if this was not available the plugs tended to oil up. In hot climates petrol vapour tended to build up in the engine compartment, particularly around the lower cylinders, and this constituted a fire hazard when starting up; it was normal practice in these circumstances to have a crewman standing by with a fire extinguisher near the open rear access doors.

A cartridge starter was supplied for use with the radial engines, and this was fired electrically from the driving compartment. The Continental engine required 20 grains of powder summer and winter, but heavier charges were necessary for the Guiberson diesel, 24 grains in summer and 30 in winter. Once the engine fired it was warmed up at 1,000rpm, at which speed the oil pressure gauge read between 65 and 90lb per square inch. Full throttle could only be applied when the oil temperature had reached 120° Fahrenheit, and normal operating temperature was between 120° and 180° with the voltmeter reading at least 14 volts and the ammeter showing 'plus'.

Being air-cooled, the radial engines gave a healthy roar when under load, muted to an irritable splutter when idling. It was suggested that before drivers switched off they should idle their engines at 400rpm for up to five minutes to permit the cylinders to cool down gently.

The twin Cadillac engines of the M5 and M5A1 employed conventional electric starters in conjunction with an automatic choke. The handbook recommended simultaneous starting followed by idling at 625rpm until normal running temperature was reached: correct oil pressure readings were 15psi for idling and 30psi for running.

As already mentioned, Marks with radial engines were fitted with synchromesh transmission, used in conjunction with a clutch; a gate separated first and reverse gears from the remainder of the box. The Hydra-matic transmission of the M5 and M5A1 was fully automatic and gear changes were controlled by the engine loading and the degree of throttle applied; reverse was manually selected.

All Marks employed controlled differential steering and the steering levers also acted as the vehicle's brakes. By pulling back simultaneously on both levers the driver was able to slow down or stop the tank, depending on the effort applied. When drawn fully back the levers could be locked in position by latches to provide a parking brake. Normally both levers were swung forward unless one or other was actually being used for steering; on the M5 and M5A1 they were mounted across the roof of the driving compartment.

Driving technique was no different from that of other tracked AFVs in that a lower gear was always selected before an obstacle, steep hill or sharp bend was reached. However, as the M5/M5A1 handbook explains, the Hydra-matic transmission also provided another facility: 'When the accelerator pedal is pushed down as far as it will go, it not only opens the throttle all the way, providing maximum engine power; it also forces the transmission control valves into the 'detent' position, which causes the transmissions to downshift from sixth to fifth speed, provided that the vehicle is travelling at less than 35 miles per hour. This downshift permits more rapid acceleration by providing a slightly lower gear ratio. This acceleration can be used to advantage in fast get-aways, passing other vehicles, gaining additional speed over viaducts, etc., and on turns.'

A fire sensor was usually fitted in the engine compartment, and two oil coolers were located on the bulkhead between the engine and fighting compartments. The M5/M5A1 also carried a single-cylinder petrol auxiliary generator, which enabled the batteries to be kept fully charged without recourse to the main engines.

The running gear was easy to maintain and complete replacement of a damaged bogie unit was a fairly simple matter. The track was adjusted by means of a nut on the trailing idler arm; this was turned clockwise, pushing out the idler and so absorbing the slack. A properly adjusted track showed a $\frac{3}{4}$in. sag midway along its top run. The track itself was of rubber block and linked-pin construction and was extremely hard-wearing. Grousers could be fitted for severe going, and when out of use these were stowed along the sides of the hull and/or turret.

Gunnery

The 37mm M5 gun carried by the M2A4 had prominent recuperators which protruded beyond the mantlet. This defect was remedied when the 37mm M6 gun was fitted to the M3 and all subsequent Marks in conjunction with an improved combination mounting. The 37mm had a calibre length of 53 and fired a 1.92lb armour-piercing shot at a muzzle velocity of 2,900 feet per second; other ammunition available included high-explosive, smoke and canister rounds.

The M3 stowed 103 rounds of main armament ammunition, as follows: 20 rounds in locker, right-hand side, against engine bulkhead; 40 rounds in locker, right-hand side, against hull wall; 43 rounds in locker, left-hand side, against engine bulkhead.

The vehicle's secondary armament consisted of .30 cal. Browning machine guns for which, in addition to standard ball ammunition, armour-piercing, tracer and incendiary rounds were also available, a typical belt mix being tracer/armour-piercing/ball/armour-piercing/tracer/armour-piercing/ball/incendiary. For an M3 with its full complement of six machine guns, including an anti-aircraft mounting, 9,850 rounds could be carried in the following manner:

1,500 rds. in locker in propeller shaft casing
4,500 rds. in 3 boxes, left rear sponson
500 rds. in box, left front sponson
1,500 rds. in 3 boxes, right rear sponson
750 rds. in box at feet of hull gunner
250 rds. in box, bow gun feed tray
250 rds. in box, right sponson gun feed tray
250 rds. in box, left sponson gun feed tray
100 rds. in box, co-ax gun feed tray
250 rds. in box, AA mounting feed tray

The two sponson guns were fired by the driver,

but were of little practical value; their mountings were fixed, and they were difficult to maintain in action. They were frequently not fitted to the M3A1 and were completely eliminated in the M3A3 design. More space was thus available for the stowage of main armament ammunition, of which 123 rounds were carried by the M3A3, M5 and M5A1.

The crew's personal weapons included pistols and a Thompson sub-machine gun (for which 750 rounds of .45 cal. ammunition was stowed in drum magazines), and 12 hand-grenades. On vehicles in British service the Thompson was more often than not replaced by a Sten from 1943.

Later Marks in British service had their turrets fitted with smoke-grenade dischargers; a Burmese variation on this theme was the welding of a standard infantry 2in. mortar to the turret, but this was rarely used.

Gun control equipment was very simple and subject to local modification. A handwheel provided elevation of $+20°$ and depression of $-10°$, and in the centre of this was a plunger which fired the main armament; an auxiliary shoulder-piece provided an alternative means of elevation. Broad traverse was obtained by the gunner turning a second handwheel with his right hand, a final lay being made with a small traverse control wheel which swung the entire gun mounting 10° right or left of centre and which incorporated a firing plunger for the co-ax machine gun.

The gyro-stabilizer had originally been developed for the Medium Tank M3, and was positioned on the turret wall close to the combination gun mount. It worked solely in the vertical plane and was unpopular with gunners, who were forced to conform to its movements by their

The turret of the M5A1 incorporated a rear overhang in which the radio was installed; and a shield-fairing covered the external turret MG pintle on the right. This model was widely used by Free French units. (RAC Tank Museum/Imperial War Museum)

auxiliary shoulder-pieces, and with commanders, who found difficulty in serving their guns while the breeches were constantly rising and falling. Such a device was not really necessary on such a small vehicle, and was not suited to the type of engagements in which it generally fought.

The power traverse system, introduced with the M3A1, employed an oil motor activated by a switch on a spade grip which the gunner turned in the required direction with his left hand; this, and an improved gun mounting, dispensed with the need for the final lay control handwheel.

The gunner's sighting telescope had a power of 1.44 with a 9° field and was marked from 600 to 3,000 yards, although in practice the 37mm's capacity to defeat German armour barely exceeded the former range. Episcopes were provided for the commander and gunner from the M3A1 onwards, and also for the driver and hull gunner on the M3A3, M5 and M5A1.

Employment

As originally conceived the US armoured division contained a recce battalion, a two-battalion infantry regiment, a towed 105mm howitzer battalion, an engineer battalion and an armoured brigade consisting of two three-battalion light tank regiments, one two-battalion medium tank regiment and one two-battalion self-propelled 105mm howitzer regiment.

However, the 1941 manoeuvres demonstrated that the infantry element of the division was too weak for its task and the establishment was re organized to include a recce battalion, two armoured regiments each of one light and two medium tank battalions, one three-battalion armoured infantry regiment in half-tracks, three self-propelled 105mm howitzer battalions and an engineer battalion. Under the old establishment the division possessed 273 light and 108 medium tanks, but the reorganization reversed these proportions to 159 light and 216 medium tanks providing a slight overall reduction.

The closing stages of the North African campaign confirmed beyond any reasonable doubt the declining importance of the light tank on Western battlefields, and thereafter it was relegated to reconnaissance and general armoured cavalry duties. None the less, in the Pacific theatre of operations the US Army and Marine Corps continued to employ light tank battalions for local support in their island-hopping campaign, as the Stuart series lent itself to amphibious operations, and opposition from the obsolete Japanese armour was minimal. The US Marine Corps' light tank battalions were divisional troops and consisted of a headquarters company

The Light Tank (Airborne) M22, seen leaving the belly of its Hamilcar glider, was used in small numbers with air landed infantry during the 1945 Rhine crossings. (RAC Tank Museum)

Converted M3A3 used as an armoured ambulance by a British armoured regiment in Italy. (Imperial War Museum)

scout company and four tank companies each with a headquarters section and three five-tank platoons; total tank strength was 72 vehicles.

The British Army was the principal beneficiary of the Lend-Lease scheme and, although disenchanted with the light tank concept, readily took the Stuart into service, since its performance fell only a little below that of its own Cruisers, and because of its proven reliability. The 4th Armoured Brigade was completely equipped with Stuarts during Operation 'Crusader', but by mid-1942 the Grant was firmly established as the 8th Army's main battle tank although the Stuart was still very actively employed in regimental light squadrons.* This tendency was accelerated by the arrival of the Sherman, but 167 Stuarts were present at Alamein, the majority with 4th Light Armoured Brigade. In Italy and North-West Europe the tank was successfully employed by the Reconnaissance Troops of armoured regiments, who much preferred it to the Daimler Scout Car. In Burma several Stuart regiments performed yeoman service from the time of the Japanese invasion until the end of the war, and the Australian Army employed a regiment in Papua.

Stuarts were also supplied in large numbers by the United States to the French, Russian and Chinese Nationalist armies, and by the British to Tito's Yugoslav partisans. After the war the vehicle served in the armies of Italy and of numerous Latin American states, and a number are believed to be still active today.

In the light of such universal service, considerations of space prevent anything more than brief mention of the tank's major achievements in the Second World War.

African Service

'Crusader'

For most of 1941 British efforts in North Africa had been concentrated upon relieving the besieged fortress of Tobruk. Two attempts, in May and June of that year, had failed because they lacked the necessary punch; but Operation 'Crusader', which commenced on 18 November, was a much larger affair involving an advance by two corps across the Egyptian frontier and a break-out by the Tobruk garrison.

On the right XIII Corps, consisting of 2nd New Zealand and 4th Indian Divisions, sup-

*For examples of Stuarts working together with Grants see Vanguard, The Lee/Grant Tanks in British Service.

ported by 1st Army Tank Brigade, would bypass the frontier defence zone and advance on Tobruk along the coast road; on the left XXX Corps, consisting of 7th Armoured and 1st South African Divisions, would advance straight across the desert in a north-westerly direction towards Sidi Rezegh and effect a junction with the Tobruk garrison at Ed Duda.

7th Armoured Division contained no less than three armoured brigades. On the left flank was the newly arrived and inexperienced 22nd (3rd and 4th County of London Yeomanry and 2nd Royal Gloucestershire Hussars) equipped entirely with Crusaders; in the centre was the veteran 7th (7th Queen's Own Hussars, 2nd and 6th Royal Tank Regiments), which possessed a motley assortment of vehicles, including 26 A10s, 71 A13s and 71 Crusaders; and on the right, covering the boundary between the two corps, was Brigadier A. H. Gatehouse's equally experienced 4th (8th King's Royal Irish Hussars, 3rd and 5th Royal Tank Regiments), each of whose regiments had a full complement of Stuarts.

Serving as a troop leader in 3 RTR was the South African test cricketer Bob Crisp, whose book *Brazen Chariots* is devoted entirely to this most gruelling and complex of desert battles.* Like everyone else in the brigade, Crisp welcomed the Stuart's speed and reliability, but was worried by its thin armour and its inability to hit hard enough:

'So I worked out a system in my troop whereby, after the target had been indicated, a more or less automatic procedure followed if the circumstances were favourable. The object was to get close enough to the enemy tank to be able to destroy it. The first order, then, was "Driver advance—flat out!" The gunner would do his best to keep his telescopic sight on the target all the time we were moving. The next order would be "Driver—halt!" As soon as the tank stopped and he was on target the gunner would fire without further command from me. The sound of the shot was the signal for the driver to let in his clutch and be off again. From stop to start it took about four seconds. All I did was to control the movement and direction of the tank. This battle

*Another personal account of the battle can be found in Cyril Joly's *Take These Men*; Joly was also serving in 3 RTR at the time.

The M8 Howitzer Motor Carriage, showing driving compartment hatches moved down onto the glacis plate. (RAC Tank Museum)

practice convinced me that in tanks that were outgunned and outarmoured, mobility was an essential element in survival.'

During the 18th the advance was uncontested, partly because the Luftwaffe's airfields were unusable after torrential rain, and partly because Rommel, preparing for a major assault on Tobruk, refused to believe that 'Crusader' was anything more than a reconnaissance in force.

About noon the following day 22nd Armoured Brigade ran into the Italian Ariete Armoured Division near Bir el Gubi and encountered unexpectedly stiff opposition; a drawn battle was fought, each side losing about 40 tanks. In the centre 7th Armoured Brigade continued its uninterrupted progress towards Sidi Rezegh, but on the right 4th Armoured Brigade was shadowed constantly by German armoured cars, which Gatehouse ordered 3 RTR to deal with. This the regiment succeeded in doing, roaring off to the north in a pursuit which brought some of its vehicles within sight of Bardia before they were recalled.

However, the armoured cars had done their work, and during the afternoon the remainder of the brigade was heavily dive-bombed and counter-attacked by a 90-tank battlegroup from 21st Panzer Division. It was the unfortunate British practice at the time not merely to deploy armoured brigades out of supporting distance of each other, but also their component regiments as well, so that in this case the weight of the attack fell mainly on 8th Hussars, who lost 20 tanks before dusk drove the two sides apart.

None the less, 3 RTR's move to the north had led General Cruewell, the DAK commander, to assume that this was the major British thrust line, and he despatched 15th Panzer Division to the south-east in a fruitless attempt to contain it. On the morning of the 20th the 4th Armoured Brigade renewed its battle with 21st Panzer Division, which swung away to the north-west; but during the afternoon 15th Panzer Division, which had discovered its mistake, also arrived on the scene, and amid confused fighting the three Stuart regiments were forced to give ground slowly. By the end of the day the brigade had only 98 operational tanks left out of the original 164, and although it claimed the destruction of some 50 Panzers, the actual number completely written off was only seven. On the other hand, it had held off both German divisions throughout the day, and the position was further secured by the arrival of 22nd Armoured Brigade from the left flank during the evening.

Both brigades looked forward to renewing the contest the following morning, but dawn revealed a desert empty of German armour. During the night Rommel had correctly appreciated that the principal British thrust was aimed at Sidi Rezegh and had ordered Cruewell to despatch both Panzer divisions there with all speed. For the next two days the 'Crusader' battlefield became an inextricable tangle of friend and foe in which formations found themselves attacking in one direction whilst defending in another. In the north the Tobruk garrison had begun to break out against opposition from 90th Light Division, which was also trying to hold Sidi Rezegh against 7th Armoured Brigade and 7th Armoured Division Support Group, who were in turn under attack from the south-east by the DAK, whose 88 and anti-tank gunners were holding up the pursuit of 22nd and 4th Armoured Brigades.

Unlike the British, the Afrika Korps fought with its armour concentrated, so that when two of 7th Armoured Brigade's regiments turned to meet its attack, one, the 7th Hussars, was all but overwhelmed, and the other, 2 RTR, was severely mauled; the third regiment, 6 RTR, was shot to pieces while supporting the Support Group's own attack. In total, 7th Armoured Brigade lost 113 of its 141 tanks. The situation was saved for the moment by the arrival of 22nd Armoured Brigade and by the open-sights firing of the Support Group's artillery and anti-tank guns.

During heavy fighting the next day the 22nd Armoured Brigade was forced away to the south and a counter-attack by 3 and 5 RTR on Sidi Rezegh airfield stalled amid the smoke, dust and confusion under the mistaken impression that it was under fire from friendly vehicles, although it did force 21st Panzer Division to retire from the immediate area. At this point control broke down and many Stuarts failed to reach the regimental rally points; 3 RTR rallied with only five, to be joined by five more at dawn, while 5 RTR rallied with 26 of the 40 with which it had begun the day.

In North-West Europe the reconnaissance troops of some British armoured regiments employed 'cut-down' M3A1s and M3A3s in preference to armoured cars. (Imperial War Museum)

Worse was to follow. 8th Hussars had not been committed to the attack on the airfield and at dusk had formed leaguer with brigade headquarters. Shortly after dark the 15th Panzer Division, which was returning to the battle after a day spent in reserve, overran the position, and by the light of flares a close-quarter fight raged for three-quarters of an hour. Some of the Hussars' Stuarts succeeded in getting clear of the mêlée, but others were captured where they

Some Stuarts were used experimentally as DD trials vehicles, but the tank lacked the heavy punch required for the rôle. (Imperial War Museum)

stood or knocked out. Fortunately Brigadier Gatehouse was with 5 RTR while this action was being fought, and escaped the destruction of his headquarters—it is some measure of the confusion in which the whole battle was fought that a few hours later Cruewell's DAK headquarters was captured by 6th New Zealand Brigade, although the general himself was absent.

Dawn on 23 November revealed the British armour in a state of total disarray. 4th Armoured Brigade was still strong in numbers but was dispersed over a wide area and effectively out of action until its command mechanism could be re-established; 7th Armoured Brigade had been reduced to a mere 15 tanks and had to be withdrawn; and the three regiments of 22nd Armoured Brigade could field only 34 tanks between them. Rommel later summed up the situation for a captured senior officer: 'What difference does it make if you have two tanks to my one, when you spread them out and let me smash them in detail? You presented me with three armoured brigades in succession.'

The effect of the previous two days' fighting had been to force the British away from the Sidi Rezegh airfield, but after destroying 5th South African Brigade on the 23rd, Rommel made a mistake which ultimately cost him the battle. On 24 November both Panzer divisions and the Ariete Armoured Division set out on what became known as the 'Dash to the Wire', which it was hoped would unnerve the British high command into ordering a general retreat across the frontier to protect its lines of communication. But the hoped-for panic failed to materialize; on the right flank XIII Corps continued to advance on Tobruk, and on the night of 26 November 4 RTR's Matildas led a meticulously planned attack which broke through to the besieged garrison.

Horrified, Rommel hurried back from the frontier and after heavy fighting was able to isolate the fortress once more, but the damage had been done. 4th and 22nd Armoured Brigades had used his absence to good purpose, repairing their cripples and breakdowns and collecting stragglers and now numbered respectively 77 Stuarts and 45 Cruisers. With these 7th Armoured Division continued to menace the Afrika Korps' desert flank, slowly writing down the German armour in a series of minor actions and threatening Rommel's own supply line by a thrust aimed at El Adem by way of Bir el Gubi.

Almost imperceptibly the initiative returned to the British. It was true that 2nd New Zealand

Division had been forced to sever its link with the Tobruk perimeter and was actually withdrawing, but 4th Indian Division had been relieved on the frontier by 2nd South African Division and was on its way forward, as were replacement tanks which ultimately raised 4th Armoured Brigade's strength to 136.

On the other side of the hill, continual attacks against British armoured and infantry formations had eroded the strength of the Panzer divisions to a dangerously low level and, thanks to the total destruction of a heavily escorted Italian convoy in a brilliant night action carried out by the Malta Striking Force, supplies of petrol and ammunition were now critical. On 3 December two columns sent to the relief of the Axis frontier garrisons at Bardia, Halfaya Pass and Sollum were ambushed and destroyed. Two days later an attempt to mount a concentrated counter-attack on 4th Armoured Brigade at Bir el Gubi was cancelled, partly because the Ariete Division failed to turn up and partly because of the death of the commander of 15th Panzer Division; 21st Panzer Division's commander had been captured a few days earlier.

Rommel now realized that to remain in the Tobruk area was to invite the annihilation of his army, and on 7 December he began to withdraw westwards towards Gazala, the first step of a well-conducted retreat that would take him out of Cyrenaica. On 16 December an attempt by 4th Armoured Brigade to cut him off at Tmimi was foiled by slow progress over difficult going and by the Stuart's greedy fuel consumption, which made a replenishment necessary and so cost further time. A second attempt at Mechili almost succeeded in catching the tail of the enemy's column, but once again petrol shortage prevented a close pursuit. The brigade continued to engage the Axis rearguard until relieved by 22nd Armoured Brigade on Christmas Day, and then returned to Egypt.

'Crusader' had been a British victory, but it had only achieved its object after a far harder fight than had been anticipated. Personnel casualties amounted to 18,000 British and 38,000 Axis, while 278 British tanks had been written off in exchange for 300 German and Italian. It had been a battle which emphasized the Stuart's vices and virtues: on the one hand its light armament, thin armour and high fuel consumption spoke for themselves; on the other, its simple robustness and reliability had been largely responsible for keeping 7th Armoured Division in

The 8th King's Royal Irish Hussars were the first British regiment equipped with Stuarts; this study of a squadron halted in the open desert gives a good impression of the unique conditions of this theatre of war. (Imperial War Museum)

the field at a time when its other two armoured brigades, equipped with Cruisers, had been reduced to a temporary state of virtual impotence.

US Army Service

'Crusader' was the last major operation in which the Stuart played a primary rôle with the British 8th Army; however, during the Anglo-American landings in Morocco and Algeria events decreed that it should once more be called upon to bear the brunt of the battle for a while. At Oran the US 1st Armored Division's 1st and 13th Armored Regiments, each equipped with one Stuart and two Lee battalions, lacked sufficient large lighters to disembark its medium tanks in the required numbers, and since the need for armour to exploit the landing was pressing it was decided to land the two light battalions and supplement their inadequate armament by providing a 75mm M3 tank destroyer element for each.

It was immediately apparent that the Vichy authorities were hostile to the landings and on 8 November 1942 the 1/1st Battalion siezed the airfield at Tafaroui, thus denying it to the French Air Force. The following day a force headed by R35 tanks was spotted approaching from the direction of Sidi-bel-Abbès, and this was intercepted and destroyed at St Lucien, the Stuarts for once outranging their opponents. (See also Vanguard 10, *Allied Tank Destroyers*, p. 15.) While this engagement was taking place the 1/13th Battalion fought its way through several roadblocks, knocking out a number of elderly armoured cars in the process, and captured the airstrip at La Senia.

On conclusion of hostilities with the French both battalions were shipped east to Tunisia, and the 1/1st played a prominent part in the attempt to sieze Tunis and Bizerta by *coup de main*, being attached to the British Blade Force on the southern flank of the thrust. After knocking out a pair of Italian self-propelled guns on 25 November the battalion launched an impertinent attack on a German battlegroup which was attempting to penetrate the Chouigui Pass. The enemy spearhead consisted of a Panzer company equipped with six PzKpfw IVF2s and a number of L/60 PzKpfw IIIs, which dealt severely with a flank attack by one Stuart company, destroying

Ease of maintenance was one of the Stuart's prime virtues. Even in the Spartan conditions of a desert workshop it was a simple matter to remove the entire turret assembly, which rested on three support rollers set 120° apart. (Imperial War Museum)

six of its 12 tanks in as many minutes. However the attack was simply a diversion for a move made by a second company round the German rear and this in turn knocked out one PzKpfw II and all the PzKpfw IVs, going on to commit mayhem among the battlegroup's lorry-born infantry. On 26 November the 1/1st crowned its achievements by storming across Djedeida airfield with the armoured cars of the Derbyshire Yeomanry, catching 37 Stuka dive-bombers actually re-arming on the ground.

Alarmed as the Germans had been by the effects of this raid, they now had sufficient troops in Tunisia to go over to the offensive themselves and during the remainder of the bitterly fought campaign the Stuarts suffered severely. The light battalions of 1st Armored Division, equipped with M3A1s, were particularly hard hit, but the M5s serving with 2nd Armored Division were not involved to the same degree.

Pacific Service

The first American tanks to see action against the Imperial Japanese Army were M3 lights of the 192nd and 194th Tank Battalions which had been shipped to Luzon, Philippine Islands, shortly before the latter's invasion and formed into a Provisional Tank Group under Brigadier General James Weaver. Neither battalion was familiar with its vehicles and both were short of vital supplies, including high-explosive ammunition and radios, but in spite of this they gave a good account of themselves when the time came.

The main Japanese landing took place in the Lingayen Gulf and was followed by an advance on Manila, supported by the Type 89 Medium and Type 95 Light tanks of the 4th and later the 7th Tank Regiments. These vehicles were badly designed, thinly armoured and poorly armed, and although their crews could show great courage and occasionally a rare flash of inspiration in local situations, they had been trained solely in simple infantry support techniques and were uneasy when confronted with enemy armour. Even so, they fought several drawn engagements with the 192nd until on New Year's Eve 1941 a Stuart company counter-attacked at Baliuag and chased 4th Tank Regiment out of the town, leaving eight of its Type 95s blazing.

After this the Japanese armour avoided contact with the Provisional Tank Group as much as possible, although the Stuarts were constantly involved in hard-fought rearguard actions as the American and Filipino troops withdrew into the Bataan peninsula. Too often their crews broke contact only to find that nervous demolition parties had blown the bridges behind them, and were forced to abandon their vehicles to avoid capture; almost one third of Weaver's 108 Stuarts fell into enemy hands in this way, and were taken into Japanese service. Latterly the Group was supplemented by M3 tank destroyers, and enjoyed its last success on 7 April 1942 when the 194th Battalion had the better of a small engagement with the 7th Tank Regiment. On the general surrender of the US forces in the Philippines the remaining Stuarts were destroyed and their crews forced to take their slim chances on the notorious Death March.

The American counter-offensive in the Pacific was not long in starting. In the South Pacific zone the 1st Marine Division landed on Guadalcanal, Solomon Islands, on 7 August 1942 and established a beachhead on the north coast between the Ilu River and Lunga Point.* This the Japanese frantically strove to eliminate, and on 21 August they launched a major attack across a sand-bar at the river mouth into the teeth of concentrated machine gun and mortar fire. Hundreds were mown down, and the survivors

*Some American accounts refer to the Ilu as the Tenaru River, which lay some way to the east; others call the area of the sand-bar Alligator Creek. See Vanguard 8, *US 1st Marine Division 1941-45*.

US Marine Corps Light Tank Battalion

Bn. HQ

- Tank Company
- Tank Company
  - HQ Section
    3 × M3 Light Tanks
  - Tank Platoon
    5 × M3 Light Tanks
  - Tank Platoon
    5 × M3 Light Tanks
  - Tank Platoon
    5 × M3 Light Tanks
- Tank Company
- Tank Company
- Scout Company
  14 × Scout Car M3A1
  12 × ¼-ton truck, recce, 4 × 4 drive

Total battalion tank strength: 72
Total company tank strength: 18
Machine guns, .30 cal. Browning, M1917A1: 28
Machine guns, .30 cal. Browning, M1919A4: 372
Machine guns, .50 cal. Browning, M2: 14
Total battalion personnel strength: 895

Stuart of 4th Light Armoured Brigade, which operated o[n] the southern sector of the Alamein front, photographed nea[r] Mt. Himeimat. In this and the previous photograph th[e] support rails for the dummy lorry canopies used at the tim[e] can be seen; they were later used for external stowage. [At] Alamein Stuarts also equipped 2nd New Zealand Division[al] Cavalry and part of 9th Australian Divisional Cavalr[y]. (Imperial War Museum)

turned and fled. The Marines counter-attacked at once, one battalion crossing the river upstream and striking the enemy flank while a platoon of 1st Marine Tank Battalion, equipped with M2A4s and M3s, drove across the sand-bar and into the heart of the position. The armoured attack, made under cover of artillery and automatic weapon fire, ploughed straight through the carnage of the failed Japanese assault until, as the Marines' divisional commander noted, 'the rear of the tanks looked like meat grinders'. Two tanks were knocked out, but the remainder pressed on to further demoralize the already broken enemy, who lost more than 800 men killed in this engagement, as opposed to 43 Americans.

The American beachhead was extended until no less than five light tank companies were available for deployment around its perimeter, and gradually a pattern began to emerge. It was soon apparent that the individual Japanese soldier was not in awe of tanks, which he would try to board with explosive devices whenever the opportunity presented itself, and to counter this it was recommended that tanks should proceed only with a close infantry escort. Employment in more open coconut plantations was preferred to that in close jungle, but repetitive use of the same routes by tanks was to be avoided, as the Japanese would mine these or move an artillery piece t[o] cover them, a lesson learned at the cost of sever[al] vehicles. It was inevitable that much of the figh[t]ing took place at close quarters against stout[ly] constructed palm-log and earth bunkers, an[d] here the Stuart's lack of firepower and limite[d] protection led to a further recommendation tha[t] in future landings by Marine Corps should b[e] supported by medium tanks, *whenever possibl[e]*. This qualification was imposed by the extremel[y] difficult nature of the going, which light tank[s] could master but which was unsuitable for th[e] heavier machines.* It is, perhaps, also wort[h] mentioning that while the explosion of the 37m[m] HE shell was indeed something of a non-even[t,] the high-velocity AP shot could be used to splinte[r] the timbers and bring down the roof over a fir[e]

*When 3rd Marine Division landed on Bougainville the followi[ng] year, its 3rd Tank Battalion was equipped with one medium and tw[o] light companies. Only the Stuarts were actively employed and the[re] is no record of the Shermans ever having left their ships. (S[ee] Plate A.)

(Left) M3A1 of 1st Armored Regt., US 1st Armd. Div.; Tunisia, December 1942. (Below) M3A1 of Company 'C', 1st Bn., 1st Armd. Regt.

M3A1 of 3rd Marine Tank Bn., US 3rd Marine Div.; Bougainville Island, November 1943

M3 of 'B' Sqn., 8th King's Royal Irish Hussars; Libya, December 1941

M3 of 'A' Sqn., 3rd Royal Tank Regt.; Libya, 194

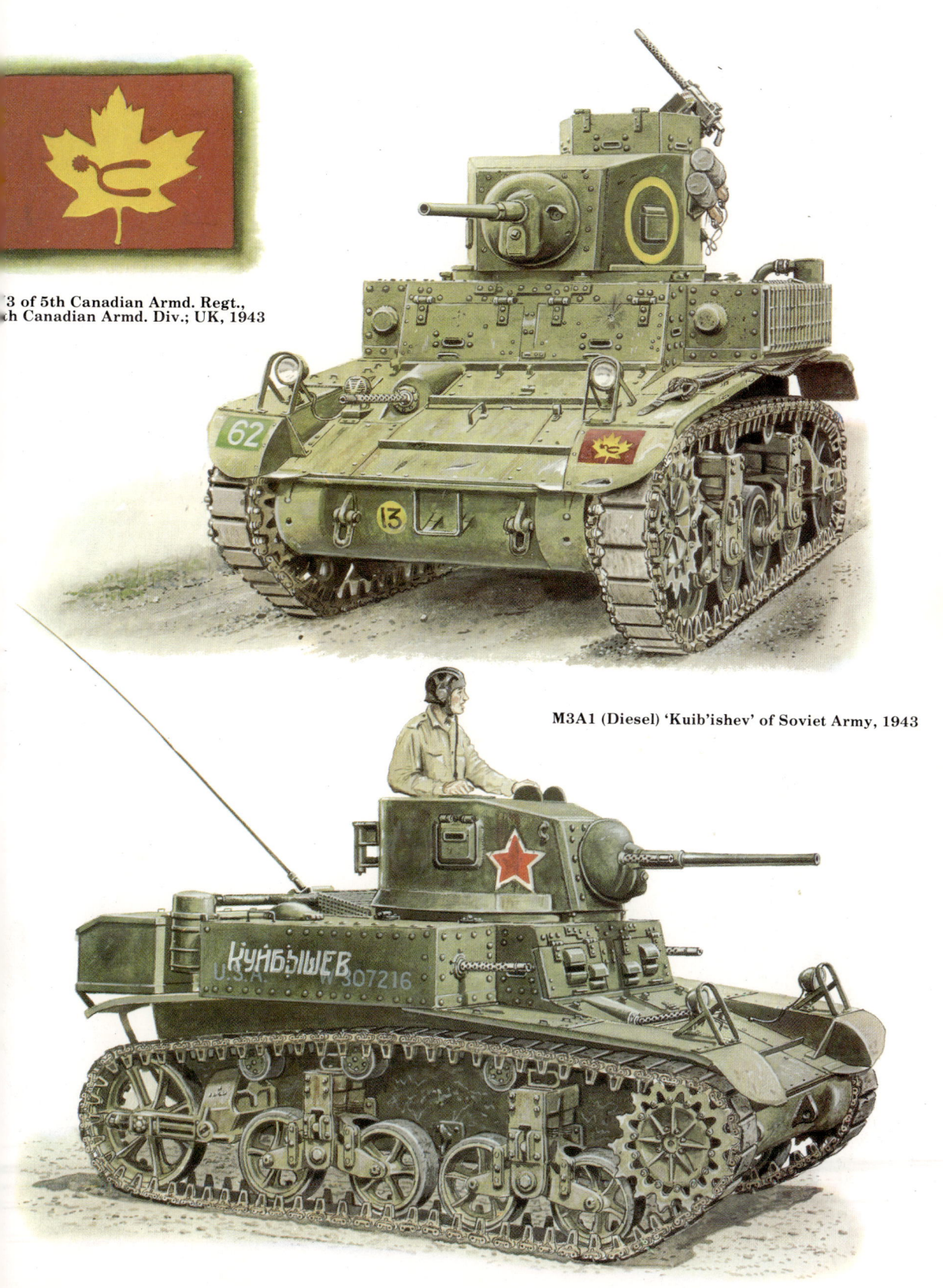

3 of 5th Canadian Armd. Regt.,
5th Canadian Armd. Div.; UK, 1943

M3A1 (Diesel) 'Kuib'ishev' of Soviet Army, 1943

M3A1 of 144th Regt. RAC, 33rd Armd. Brigade; France, summer 1944

M5A1 of 3rd Scots Guards, 6th Guards Tank Bde.; North-West Europe, early 1945

M3A1 of 'A' Sqn., 7th Indian Light Cavalry; Burma, 1944-45

M3A3 of Yugoslav 1st Partisan Tank Brigade, 1944-45

M5A1 of 1st French Armd. Div. (1ᵉʳ D B); Italy, 1944–45;
(Right) Brigadier-chef of 12ᵉ Chasseurs d'Afrique, 2ᵉ D B;
Paris, August 1944

M8 Howitzer Carriage of
1ᵉʳ REC, 5ᵉ D B; France, 1944

F

M3A3 Stuart V turret interiors, looking forward and (below) to rear. See key on on p. 25.

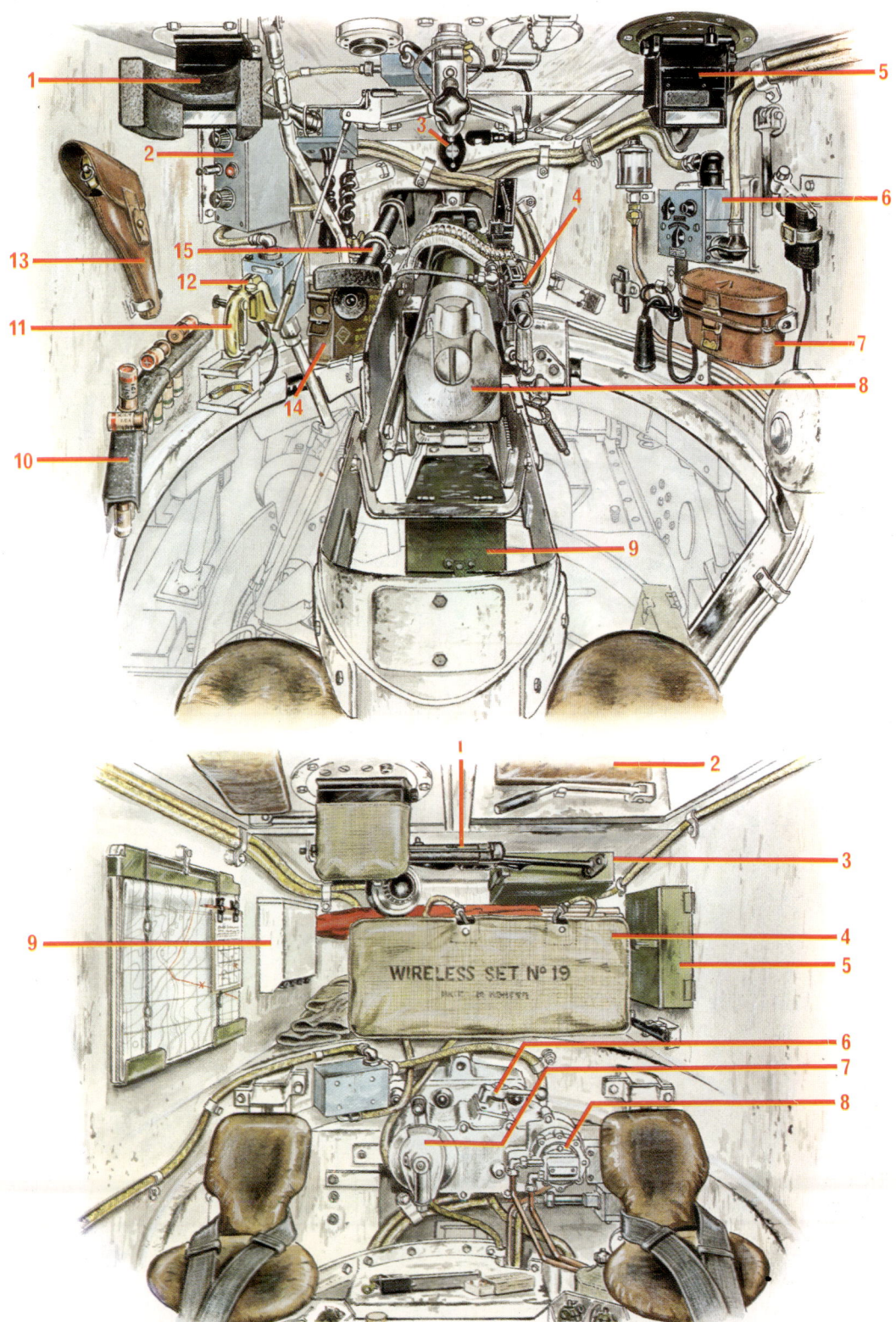

G

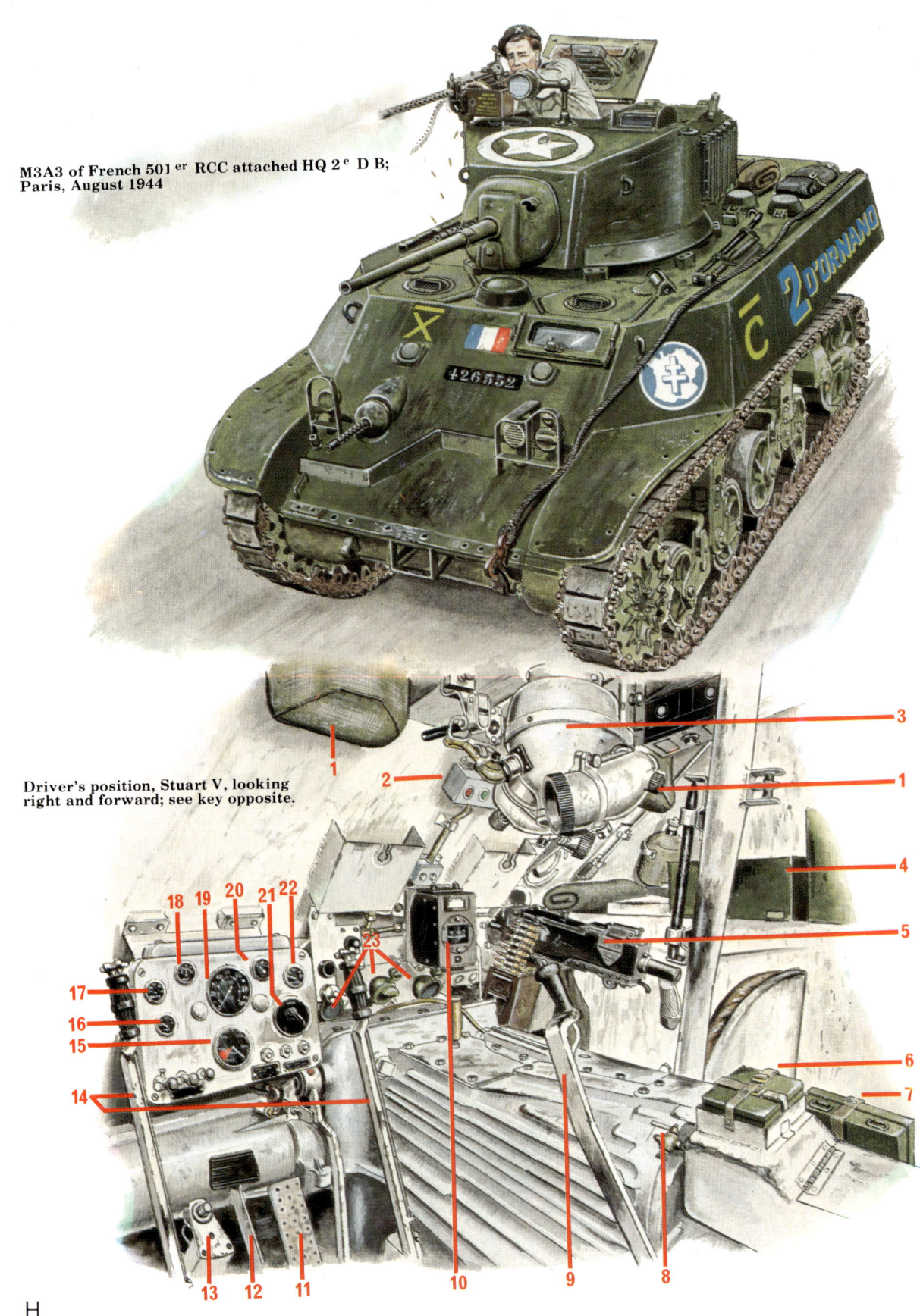

M3A3 of French 50J er RCC attached HQ 2 e D B; Paris, August 1944

Driver's position, Stuart V, looking right and forward; see key opposite.

Plate G (top): M3A3 Stuart V turret interior, looking forward:
1. Periscope M4 (with telescope, M40)
2. Stabilizer/recoil controls
3. Hull compass
4. Co-axial .30 cal. MG
5. Periscope M6
6. W/T and intercom controls
7. Binocular stowage
8. 37mm gun breech in M23 combination mount
9. Stowage for 8 rounds 37mm ammunition
10. Stowage for 12 signal cartridges
11. Gunner's power traverse control
12. Gun triggers
13. Signal pistol stowage
14. Co-axial MG ammunition box
15. Sighting telescope

Plate G (bottom): M3A3 turret, looking to rear:
1. 9mm Sten sub-machine gun (British vehicles)
2. Left-hand hatch, open
3. Stowage for tools, MG spares, etc.
4. W/T set
5. Spare periscope stowage
6. Traverse mechanism clutch lever
7. Manual traverse crank
8. Hydraulic traverse mechanism
9. Stowage for 9 magazines, Sten or Thompson SMGs

Plate H (bottom): M3A3 Stuart V driver's position, looking right and forward:
1. Periscopes M6, with canvas covers
2. Intercom
3. Extractor fan assembly and trunking
4. Stowage, spare periscope and heads
5. .30 cal. Browning MG with ammunition box, and bag for spent cartridges
6. Stowage, W/T spares
7. First aid box
8. Oil circulation test cock mounted on transmission housing
9. Gear lever
10. Compass
11. Foot throttle
12. Clutch pedal
13. Siren button
14. Track steering levers
15. Tachometer
16. Engine oil temperature gauge
17. Engine oil pressure gauge
18. Ammeter
19. Speedometer
20. Voltmeter
21. Magneto switch
22. Transmission oil pressure gauge
23. Spare headlights and blackout light

lit, and the canister round was extremely useful in sweeping surrounding tree-tops clear of snipers and in breaking up mass infantry attacks.

These lessons were being learned simultaneously in MacArthur's South-West Pacific zone, where Australian and American troops were locked in combat with the Japanese in northern Papua. By December 1942 the enemy thrust on Port Moresby had been defeated and what remained of the Japanese force was firmly entrenched along the coast from Cape Endaiadere to Buna, holding off unsupported infantry attacks to such good effect that tanks became an absolute necessity for breaching the impenetrable field defences.

The going was far worse than in the Solomons, and was in fact so bad that the Australian official historian commented that the tank crews faced a prospect that could only be justified by a desperate need'. Behind the beach lay a belt of swamp, cut up by tidal creeks and backed by jungle; plantations and two derelict airstrips provided firmer ground but were pitted with treacherous bog-holes, while visibility was reduced by tall kunai grass, which also concealed the stumps of trees which the Japanese had felled to construct their bunkers and on which a vehicle could belly as easily as on any purpose-built tank trap. In such circumstances detailed route reconnaissance was mandatory before each operation, but even this failed to keep the tanks out of trouble where drivers were blinded by vegetation and commanders were forced to operate closed down because of enemy fire.

The tanks employed were Stuart M3s manned by the Australian 2/6th Armoured Regiment, which had trained for the North African desert but which suddenly found itself in a totally un-

'Exe', the RSO's Stuart of 5th RTR in 4th Light Armoured Brigade. The name and HQ diamond are painted in a dark purple-blue on plain sand yellow. (Imperial War Museum)

familiar environment. Seven tanks took part in an attack at Cape Endaiadere on 18 December and slowly ground their way into the Japanese position, beating down the fire of bunkers and automatic weapon pits. The enemy responded by swamping several vehicles under a wave of infantry, who fired into the vision slits and burned out one Stuart by planting a magnetic mine against its armour. A second tank was set on fire after it had bellied on a tree stump, but the Australian infantry swept the intruders off the remaining Stuarts with their own fire, and the advance continued until the firm going gave way to bog.

This sort of fighting continued until the last Japanese positions were stormed in mid-January. The Stuarts had provided a key to the tactical problem, but they and their crews had suffered severely from the point-blank fire of totally concealed 37mm anti-tank and 3in. anti-aircraft guns. The inevitable conclusions were drawn that light tanks were unsuitable for such close-quarter engagements, although it was freely admitted that the Stuart was the only tank in the Australian armoury which could have operated in such conditions.

On 30 November 1943 the US 2nd Marine Division launched its assault landing on the tiny 300-acre island of Betio in the Tarawa atoll. In 76 hours of the most concentrated and savage fighting of the Second World War the Japanese garrison of 4,700 men was all but exterminated at a cost of 985 Marines killed and 2,193 wounded. Armoured support for the operation was provided by the 1st Marine Amphibious Corps Tank Battalion, equipped with two companies of Stuart M3A1s and one company of Shermans.

'The two terrain features which caused great difficulties to the infantry likewise proved to be an impediment in bringing tanks into action. The reef which extended roughly parallel to the shore along the landing beaches precluded the possibility of getting the LCTs near the beach proper. It was necessary for crewmen to disembark at the reef, wade ashore over the partly submerged coral shelf, and pick out a path that could be followed by the tanks. During this phase of the operation one tank was lost as a result of falling into a hole in the coral.

'It will be remembered that along almost the entire beach there had been built a sea-wall several feet high, strongly constructed of coconut logs. The distance between this wall and the water's edge was only a few feet and the infantry was, for a time, pinned down in this narrow strip by fire from enemy emplacements inland. There was, at all times, congestion on the beach.'*

As the beach was covered with wounded, the tanks were forced to roam the shallows in their search to find a way inland, and several more were lost in submerged shell-holes. Eventually seven forced their way through a gap which had been blown in the sea-wall and began tackling the enemy strongpoints, their fire supplemented by two 75mm M3 tank destroyers. This combination of direct gunfire and the suicidal bravery of Marines using explosive charges against the bunker fire-slits broke the back of the defence. (Arising from the Tarawa operations was a recommendation that one light tank per platoon should be equipped as a flame-thrower. The USMC employed Stuart flame-throwers in subsequent operations in the Marianas, Saipan, Tinian and on Guam.)

The Stuart M5A1 made its Pacific début during 4th Marine Division's assault on the

*Armored Cavalry Journal, Sept/Oct 1946.

Kwajalein atoll in January/February 1944, and on 18 February tanks from the same unit landed to support the 22nd Marine Regiment in its capture of Eniwetok:

'The tanks were indispensable here. They were the only things that could move up to the log bunkers, hidden in the foliage, and smash them quickly. But on Eniwetok Island their danger was greater than before. At the southern end of the island the Japs had 77mm guns, originally installed as coast defence pieces. These were turned to duel with the advancing tanks and one scored a direct hit, killing the crew and effectively putting the tank out of action.

'Night brought no let-up for the tank men. They went on and on in the unrelenting process of pushing the Japs toward both ends of the island. You could see their cannon spitting jets of flame in the night as they hammered at pillboxes and snuffed out machine gun nests. At night, destroyers moved along the shores, illuminating them with dazzling white lanes from searchlights. Through their beams rumbled the dark, massive bulks of the tanks, moving steadily against the enemy.

'It is incredible what men can stand in battle.

M3 in Free French service parading in front of Allied commanders at Kano, Nigeria. We have been unable to identify the unit; the tank is overall olive green with a white Cross of Lorraine on each side of the turret, the name 'Poitou' in white thick/thin capitals high and central on the hull side, and a large red heart on a white square painted to almost the full depth of the hull, centred on its height, forward of the muffler. (Imperial War Museum)

The men in those tanks had not slept for four nights. They were filthy, tired, dazed and hot. Their heads rang from the constant firing of the tanks' cannon and machine guns. They had eaten nothing but a little K-ration and had been drinking almost steaming hot water. The tanks themselves were on the verge of breaking down. There was no time for service or repair; the only thing they stopped for was fuel. Then they went lumbering up into the Jap positions to resume their deadly fire.

'The battle for Eniwetok Island lasted for three days. Men who had fought in both places said the terrain and the enemy were worse than at Guadalcanal. If it had not been for the small group of tanks, the battle might have lasted for weeks. They broke up the Jap jungle lines and almost literally carved paths for the foot troops to follow.'*

Stuarts also fought, *inter alia*, in support of the dismounted US 1st Cavalry Division during the 25-day campaign to secure the Admiralty Islands, and the following extract from an after-action report illustrates the degree to which infantry/tank co-operation had become an instinctive drill by the first quarter of 1944.

'D+6. Three light tanks arrived. They went into action immediately with 12th Cavalry to clear Salami Plantation on Los Negros Island. The first contact they made with the enemy was in the vicinity of some buildings near the beach on the west coast. There were several pillboxes in the area. Canister was fired into the buildings at ranges up to 50 yards. 37mm HE was used on pillbox slits. Due to their camouflage, it was necessary to get within 30 yards of the bunkers. If the slit was not visible to the tank gunner but was to the ground troops near the tank, the latter would indicate its location by tracer. Some machine gun fire was employed but not as much as in later actions. This engagement lasted only about one hour.'**

Burma

On the day that Rommel finally abandoned the siege of Tobruk the Japanese attacked Pearl

**Marine Corps Gazette*, August 1944.

**Report No. 62, Army Ground Forces Board, South-West Pacific Area, 27 April 1944.

M5A1 of 1ᵉʳ Escadron, 1ᵉʳ Régiment de Marche de Spahis Marocains, 2ᵉ Division Blindée parading in triumph down the Champs-Elysées, 26 August 1944. Below the bridge disc on the glacis are the French tricolour outlined in yellow, and white number '420463'. The yellow regimental code 'R' between two yellow bars is on a dark blue square. The divisional sign is painted on the right side of the hull. The Spahis wear scarlet sidecaps, and American overalls. (Daniel Ambrogi)

Harbor, and so initiated their series of runaway victories in the Far East. In Malaya they successfully used tanks in circumstances which the British Imperial General Staff had pronounced impossible, and to counter this threat the 7th Armoured Brigade, now consisting of 7th Hussars and 2 RTR, was hastily re-equipped with Stuarts and despatched from Egypt.

On receipt of the news that Singapore had fallen, the brigade was diverted to Rangoon, the Japanese also having invaded Burma on 15 January 1942. A scratch defence line along the Sittang River was not expected to hold, and immediately after landing 2 RTR was ordered into a blocking position in the Payagyi/Waw area. Here for several days the regiment was involved in patrol activity until in the misty dawn light of 4 March it was assailed by a large force specially equipped with explosive pole charges. The Japanese timing was unfortunate, for at that moment the 7th Hussars were moving up to relieve 2 RTR and the infantrymen thus found themselves confronted by two Stuart regiments. Considerable execution was done by the tanks' machine guns, and the relief continued without undue interruption.

Balked on one of their major axes of advance the Japanese brought up some of their own tanks the following day. Their crews showed not the slightest tactical sense, and they were knocked out before they realized what was happening. The Hussars resisted further attempts to dislodge them and would have been quite happy to remain in the position had not events elsewhere compelled their withdrawal through Pegu to rejoin the brigade at Hlegu. Pegu was in enemy hands and the Stuarts were forced to fight their way through—in one incident a Japanese officer leapt from his horse onto a tank, hoping to kill the commander with his sword, but was removed by the latter using a hammer against his head to some effect.

It was now apparent that Rangoon could not be held, and it was decided that the army should withdraw northwards into India. The move was almost stopped dead in its tracks by a road-block established at Taukkyon on 7 March, but this was abandoned during the night in complete ignorance of the fact that the Army Commander, General H. R. L. G. Alexander and most of the British troops in Burma lay trapped to the south.

Thereafter, the two Stuart regiments alternated as rearguard during the long retreat. The 7th Hussars were committed to an ill-advised counter-attack south of Prome, little realizing that the enemy had used his legendary jungle mobility to establish further road-blocks behind them. Ten tanks had to be abandoned when the regiment fought its way out across country, and these were later recovered and employed by the Japanese.

On 16 April the rearguard was again overtaken at Yenangyaung. The retreating column was broken up into several sections and 2 RTR found themselves fighting the same sort of multi layer battle in which they had been involved at Sidi Rezegh. Relief appeared in the form of the Chinese 38th Division and the situation was restored after several days' hard fighting; this was, in fact, the only occasion in history when British armour fought under the direct command of a Chinese GOC.

Near Meiktila a patrolling Hussar troop ran

head-on into a Japanese motorized infantry convoy on 25 April, running the length of the column twice and slaughtering the terrified passengers as they scrambled from their burning vehicles. Two days later 2 RTR fought a day-long holding action at Wundwin against enemy infantry and armour. On the 29th the Hussars' 'B' Squadron beat off an infantry attack at Kyaukse with the massed fire of their machine guns, and then supported a counter-attack by the Gurkhas of 48 Brigade; one Gurkha died, but 300 Japanese bodies were counted on the hill where the action had taken place.

In other campaigns the enemy's skill in isolating and overwhelming sections of the Allied armies had worked well, but in Burma the majority of such attempts were defeated by the ever-present Stuarts. On one occasion, using some of the Hussars' tanks lost at Prome, an attempt was made to infiltrate the rearguard as it moved off in the darkness, but this was quickly detected by 2 RTR and summarily dealt with. In another incident, several Hussar vehicles were assailed at close quarters with frangible glass grenades containing liquid hydrogen cyanide; these produced little practical return, but are the first recorded instances of AFVs being attacked by purely chemical means.

On the night of 29 April the rearguard crossed the Irrawaddy by the great Ava bridge, which was blown up behind them. The impression of safety was, however, both short-lived and illusory, for the Japanese were already pushing up the Chindwin and had already landed on the army's flank at Monywa. 7th Hussars were sent into the area at once, the journey involving a road march of 140 miles, and successfully extricated an infantry brigade which had been trapped. 2 RTR then took over as rearguard, covering the army's withdrawal through Yeu to Kalewa, where it was to cross the Chindwin into India.

Civilian ferry boats were used to complete the evacuation. At this point the Chindwin was only 400 yards wide, but the only landing on the Indian bank was four miles upstream. 7th Hussars put one of their tanks on a raft which was

M3s of the US 70th Tank Bn. training in Iceland, April 1942; this unit later fought in North Africa and Normandy. (US Army)

An M3A1 of 1st Armored Regt., US 1st Armored Div. photographed in Tunisia, December 1942, in company with a Lee and a half-track; all are liberally smeared with pale mud as camouflage. (RAC Tank Museum)

towed across behind a ferry, but the passage took so long that the vessel's crew threatened to strike if asked to repeat the operation. As a result of this 7th Armoured Brigade was forced to destroy its tanks to prevent their use by the enemy, and this was done so thoroughly that when the British returned to the site more than two years later not one vehicle had been moved. 'C' Squadron 7th Hussars fought a last action on 10 May to prevent the Japanese closing in on the evacuation area, and then its tanks, too, were reduced to scrap by their own crews.

There is no doubt whatever that had it not been for 7th Armoured Brigade very few of the British and Indian troops in Burma would have reached India. For their part, veterans of both regiments are agreed that they could not have performed their difficult task in any other tank than the Stuart; and the Great Retreat, in which most vehicles covered 1,000 miles on their own tracks, remains the design's most impressive achievement.*

The one tank which reached India was eventually issued to the 7th Light Cavalry, who removed its turret and enclosed the fighting compartment with a framework of anti-grenade netting. In this form it served on throughout the Burma war as a command vehicle, being christened *The Curse of Scotland* by the commanding officer, Lt.-Col. Jack Barlow, no doubt to the annoyance of sentimental adherents to the lost Jacobite cause.

7th Light Cavalry was a regular Indian regiment whose men had been recruited from among the sub-continent's traditional martial races. They enjoyed fighting, were good at it, and possessed a natural cavalry dash. Whatever their race, communication with their British officers was in Urdu, the Indian Army's *lingua franca*.

When, early in 1944, the Japanese surrounded the British IV Corps at Imphal, the regiment formed part of 254 Indian Tank Brigade, and throughout the siege fought in numerous engagements around the perimeter in which quarter was neither asked for nor expected by either side.** Of these one of the most spirited was that fought by 'A' Squadron on 22 March.

'At 0600hrs No. 2 Troop plus the remaining tank of No. 1 Troop went into the attack on the enemy position now called Fir Tree Hill, working in conjunction with 10th Gurkha Rifles. The attack was a complete success. The position was overrun and numerous Japs were killed. In the early stages of the action Jemadar Ram Gopal's tank was pierced by a solid shot from a Jap 75mm and the gunner killed. Nevertheless the tank was fought as well as could be and was not ordered

---

*For a full account of the brigade's part in the retreat, and other tank battles in Burma, see the author's *Tank Tracks to Rangoon*, published by Robert Hale.

**The other units in 254 Brigade were 3rd Carabiniers and Y Squadron 150 Regiment RAC—see Vanguard 6, *The Lee/Grant Tanks in British Service.*

back until success had been obtained.

'Captain Cole also had a little difficulty. Whilst standing on the top of a bunker, a 4in. mortar-bomb struck his engine plate, making a large hole in the plate and setting the tank on fire. With the aid of the main fire extinguisher he put out the fire and carried on with the action. Later a Jap crawled behind the tank and threw in a fire bomb, again setting the tank on fire; he was killed by Captain Cole, who shot him with his pistol through the pistol port. Having no other means at his disposal with which to put the fire out, he ordered the crew to bale out, at the same time giving them all covering fire with the co-ax Browning until they were clear, then baled out himself.

'Risaldar Bharat Singh did extremely well, taking over the troop whilst engaged in the action and in general killing every Jap that came his way. It was quite easy to tell where his tank had been operating as his trail was littered at short intervals with piles of 37mm empty cases. He is considered to be the fastest loader in the squadron. [Bharat Singh commanded the No. 1 Troop tank, and for him this was a grudge fight; some days earlier the troop had lost two of its tanks and the Japanese had butchered their crews, only one man escaping to tell the tale.]

'The whole of the engagement was a grand sight, and the training with the infantry which had been done previously proved its worth. It was great fun to stand literally 10 feet away from the slit of a bunker and pump every available round into it; also to run backwards and forwards over the bunker until the whole thing finally collapsed.'

Damaged M5A1 of US 14th Armored Div. photographed in Lorraine, 10 January 1945. A German bomb struck a case of mines lying near the tank, and the explosion has ripped off both the drive sprocket and the final drive half-shaft. (US Army)

Some weeks later the regiment's 'B' Squadron was detailed for a spectacular attack on a feature known as The Beacon. This involved a climb of 1,700 feet up an extremely steep hillside, and for much of the way the Stuarts were winched up the slope by a D8 tractor driven by Trooper Thomson from the brigade's Forward Delivery Squadron, who continued to perform his slow, methodical work in complete disregard of the fire being directed at him from the crest. At length four tanks reached the summit, which they proceeded to clear in a fight carried on amid rain and mountain mist which reduced visibility to five yards. One tank bogged down and another lost a track on a mine, and as resources could not be diverted to their recovery they were abandoned after the action; Manipur being one of the world's remoter areas, it is more than likely that they are to be found there still, less their armament.

On 22 June 'C' Squadron, having spent several days fighting their way through the northern rim of the Japanese lines, broke out and raced up the Kohima road to meet the Lees of 149 Regiment RAC coming south; British XXXIII Corps had finally broken through and the siege was over. Decimated by battle casualties, disease and starvation, the Japanese were in full retreat to the Chindwin, leaving 55,000 dead behind them.

A second Stuart regiment, the newly raised 45th Cavalry, had protected XXXIII Corps' lines of communication during the battle to penetrate the Japanese defences at Kohima, while on the North Burma Front Stilwell's offensive down the Hukaung and Mogaung valleys was led by an M3A3 battalion known as the Chinese 1st Provisional Tank Unit.

The 7th Light Cavalry took part in the pursuit across the Chindwin with XXXIII Corps, and then fought in the bloody battles which took place around the latter's Irrawaddy bridgeheads. At Talingon the enemy's literal obedience to his orders was fully exploited in a series of infantry/tank attacks which lasted for 10 days. Each day the garrison would be exterminated in their bunkers, and then the village would be abandoned; and each night the Japanese would obligingly provide a fresh garrison to man positions, the location of which the tank crews soon knew by heart.

'By 26 February 1945 the number of Jap dead was over 500; 16 officers' swords, two 75s and a dozen machine guns were captured, and among the dead were two Jap battalion commanders. A Jap captured later stated that he was the only survivor, and that it had been hell.

'Talingon had broken the back of the Jap resistance, and at Ywabo North, after a terrific artillery barrage, they ran when we attacked. But they did not run fast enough for No. 3 Troop, accompanied by a platoon of Pathans, who chased them and caught them just short of their next position. They were routed out of bush and tree and over 30 met their end as they made a last dash for safety. They ran again a couple of days later when we attacked Ywabo South, where our only casualty was a broken track. From Ywabo South we pushed across the dry barren hills to Magyi and Kanma. Here, whilst Harpy pushed into the village, No. 3 Troop was sent to play hide-and-seek amongst the palm-trees with a couple of 75s. Jemadar Man Singh's tank was hit twice and he won an MC for directing fire onto the gun's position though he was painfully wounded in the chest. He was evacuated by

Almost buried in hitch-hiking infantry, a Stuart advances into Germany. (USAMHI)

a fearless American Field Service man—a force for which we had much respect.'

Already bled white by the Irrawaddy battles, the Japanese army disintegrated as a result of Slim's master stroke at Meiktila with IV Corps. In the dash to Rangoon which concluded the campaign 'A' and 'B' Squadrons formed the advance guard along IV Corps' axis through Toungoo, Payagyi and Pegu, working with the Humber armoured cars of 16th Light Cavalry, while 'C' Squadron and 11th Cavalry's Daimlers led XXXIII Corps' advance down the left bank of the Irrawaddy.

In Burma, as elsewhere in the Far East, the need for tanks to have a close infantry escort during bush or village fighting was quickly appreciated, and several Bombay Grenadier battalions were specially trained for this work. The grenadiers earned the admiration of all who came in contact with them, but even so Japanese suicide squads would occasionally break through and attempt to place explosive devices on the engine decks, and to counter this a stout wire grille was fitted, the effect being to disperse the worst effects of the explosion above the armour plate.

The Plates

A1: *M3A1 of 1st Bn, 1st Armored Regiment, 1st US Armored Division; Tunisia, December 1942*

The tank is painted overall Olive Drab, camouflaged on the spot by a heavy application of pale clay mud, a common practice in 1st Armored Division; some Stuarts, Lees and half-tracks were almost covered with it, while others had carefully applied geometric patterns. The star and turret band were used as national insignia in this campaign and in this instance were painted in yellow; as the campaign progressed this was sometimes changed to a pale blue to

A heavily-stowed M5A1, a Sherman platoon and an M8 armoured car are all visible in this set-piece study of the final advance into the Reich. (USAMHI)

defeat the type of film being used by German air-photo recce aircraft. The individual tank number was marked in black on the star. The vehicle has a welded hull and is fitted with jettison tanks; it will be noted that the apertures for the sponson machine guns have been blanked off.

A2: *M3A1 of Company 'C', 1st/1st Armored Regiment, 1st US Armored Division; Tunisia, December 1942*

This vehicle was knocked out during the December fighting. The star carries the vehicle number with three red bars indicating that it belonged to the 3rd Platoon. Close to the left sponson machine gun mounting is the Company 'C' symbol, a bar with a disc above its right end. The 1st/1st's HQ Company had the disc level with the bar at its left end; Company 'A' showed the disc above the left end, while Company 'B' displayed it above the centre of the bar. 'Rebel' is the crew's choice of name, but has been painted in the then orthodox yellow. The American national flag was carried on the hull sides of most US AFVs during the *Torch* landings, but was soon smeared with mud after the first experience of combat, and eventually disappeared.

A3: *M3A1 of 3rd Marine Tank Bn., 3rd US Marine Division; Bougainville Island, November 1943*

Photographic evidence confirms that these were the only markings carried by this vehicle which, it will be noted, has a welded hull. The turret insignia, showing company and platoon markings, was unique to USMC tank battalions.

Splendidly domestic study of a Marine crew at work on the final drive and suspension of their M3 'somewhere in the South Pacific' early in 1943. The USMC employed its own system of markings, but the original US Army serial 'W-304169' in drab blue can still be seen on the sponson. (USMC)

M5A1s of the US Army's 754th Tank Bn. supporting the 129th Infantry on Bougainville, Solomon Islands, March 1944. On the left can be seen the upper layer of one of the formidable Japanese palm-log bunkers. (US Army)

B1: *M3 of 'B' Sqn., 8th (King's Royal Irish) Hussars, British 7th Armoured Division; Egypt, late summer 1941*

The camouflage of desert sand, stone grey and dark green, applied diagonally in large straight-edged areas, is typical of the period. The white/red/white recognition flash, introduced during the First World War, was also used by British tanks during the early years of the Second World War, and is seen here painted on the turret side, centrally on the front plate and on the sides of the sand shields, well forward. The divisional sign (inset) can be seen on the leading edge of the left-hand sand shield; the photograph on which our painting is based reveals no evidence of the regiment's tactical number. The 'B' Squadron square, in yellow, is painted over the turret recognition flash; as senior regiment in their brigade the 8th were entitled to mark all their vehicles in red, but obviously preferred the internal alternative of marking 'A' Sqn. in red, 'B' in yellow and 'C' in blue. The regiment had a strong hunting tradition and the name BELLMAN commemorates a famous foxhound. The WD number 'T.28037' is displayed on a panel of the original Olive Drab finish on the hull sides. The commander wears the obsolete American tank crew helmet in russet leather, issued with the tanks and widely worn by this unit for a while. The officer on the left is taken from another photograph and is seen at a chilly early morning briefing; he wears the green and gold 'tent hat' unique to 8th Hussar officers, a *poshteen* or Afghan coat and over it a standard issue leather trench-jerkin, together with the *de rigueur* corduroy trousers and crêpe-soled chukkah-boots so popular with old desert hands.

B2: *M3 of 3 Troop, 'A' Squadron, 3rd Royal Tank Regiment; Cyrenaica, January 1942*

An unusual application of the same basic camouflage pattern. The stone grey is still painted in large, straight, diagonal areas, but the green has been added over both stone grey and basic sand in wide random blotches. The regiment's tactical number, '86' at this period, is marked on the left-hand sand shield, with the divisional sign on the right-hand sand shield. The 'A' Squadron triangle and troop number on the turret are both painted in yellow, confirming that 3 RTR, as second-senior regiment of their brigade, conformed to the official system of internal marking. The vehicle name COLUMBIA IV and WD number 'T.37764' are painted in black. Other points of interest include the lights protected by old steel helmets; the canvas gun cover tucked behind the mantlet in an attempt to foil

35

the all-penetrating sand; and the method of tying down the aerial.

C1: *M3 of 'C' Squadron, 5th Canadian Armoured Regiment (8th Princess Louise's New Brunswick Hussars), 5th Canadian Armoured Division; United Kingdom, 1943*

The regiment's tactical number '62' is painted in white on a green square, denoting that it belongs to the junior armoured brigade of a two-brigade division. The divisional sign (inset) is painted on the left-hand track-guard; other markings include the squadron insignia and bridge classification. A pair of British smoke grenade dischargers has been welded to the turret.

C2: *M3A1 (Diesel), Red Army, 1943*

Original Olive Drab colour scheme with blue stencils 'U.S.A.' and 'W-307216' still visible on hull sides, with the name '*Kuib'ishev*' over-painted in Cyrillic script in white. The white-outlined red star is seldom seen other than on AFVs supplied under Lend-Lease, and is a defence against faulty identification of an unfamiliar

The additional armour girdle which the Royal Australian Armoured Corps normally welded around the turret ring of its tanks to prevent jamming by shell splinters and small arms fire can be seen in this photograph of Stuarts of 'B' and 'C' Sqns., 2/6th Armoured Regt., which fought in Papua in December 1942–January 1943. The 2/6th was raised from the old 6th Light Horse, and what appears to be the latter's crest can just be seen on the right front track-guard, as viewed. (US Army)

type by other Red Army units. Considerable numbers of Stuarts were supplied to Russia; the provision of tank radios with them went some way to solving the ever-present radio famine, but the technical difficulties of replacing the 37mm gun with a more powerful Russian weapon, common practice with Lend-Lease AFVs, could not be satisfactorily solved. The vehicle is slightly unusual in that the entire complement of machine guns has been retained.

D1: *M3A1, Recce Troop, 144 Regiment RAC, 33rd Armoured Brigade; Normandy, summer 1944*

By this stage of the war many British regiments used large individual numbers on the turret sides, or rear in the case of larger vehicles, the Stuarts of Recce Troop being numbers 1–11. The regiment's tactical number '174' can be seen in white on a red square on the right-hand track-guard. The brigade's original rôle as a Tank Brigade is commemorated in the green/black diabolo (inset) seen on the left-hand track-guard, but in Normandy it fought as an independent armoured brigade before joining 79th Armoured Division and being re-equipped with Buffaloes. 144 Regiment was formed from a battalion of the East Lancashire Regiment and was re-designated 4 RTR on 1 March 1945, replacing the original 4th which had been lost at the fall of Tobruk in 1942. The photograph on which the painting is based was taken not long after the regiment had landed in Normandy: witness the lower section of the deep-wading trunk still in place, covered with tank sheets and miscellaneous stowage.

D2: *M5A1, Recce Troop, 3rd Bn. The Scots Guards, 6th Guards Tank Brigade; North-West Europe, early 1945*

The tactical number '53' with the Army troops white bar below does not conform with other sources on 3rd Scots Guards, but our source photograph shows it quite clearly, together with the unmistakable cap star. The name THE BLACK BEAR, the title of a popular pipe march, is taken from the regiment's own list of Stuarts used by Recce Troop. It is possible, but not likely, that the HQ Sqn. diamond appeared in blue on the turrets of some vehicles. A broad air-recognition symbol has been painted on the turret roof. A pair of smoke-grenade dischargers has been welded to the AA machine gun pintle fairing, and additional stowage boxes, made from ammunition containers, to the glacis and catwalks.

E1: *M3A1 of 3 Troop, 'A' Squadron, 7th Light Cavalry, Indian Armoured Corps; Burma, 1944–45*

This vehicle was commanded by Captain Harry Travis, to whom we are grateful for details of its markings. Finished in overall drab-green, it has the name THE HAMMER OF THOR lettered in white capitals around the mantlet; other names known to have been used by the regiment and painted in the same position are OM (a Hindu prayer), SHER (Tiger) and CAWNPORE. The 7th was often at close quarters with the Japanese, who made desperate attempts to place hollow-charge ex-

An extremely rare picture of 2nd RTR 'in harbour' during the retreat from Burma in 1942. The Stuart had been shipped from Egypt in such haste that they fought throughout the campaign in their sand and light stone desert colour scheme. Further photographic evidence confirms that 7th Armoured Bde. had a number of M2A4s in addition to their M3s. (Courtesy 2nd Royal Tank Regiment)

plosive devices on the glacis and engine deck; a wire grille was fitted over both to dissipate the main force of the explosion before it reached the armour plate. The grille obscures the markings on the glacis plate, which are shown inset as viewed from the front of the tank; left, the regiment's tactical number in white on the IAC's scarlet and yellow square, and right, the insignia of 14th Army; these signs were repeated on the rear of the vehicle. The turret markings are in yellow, 7th Light Cavalry being the second senior regiment of 254 Indian Tank Brigade. An additional stowage bin has been welded to the right-hand track-guard. Personnel of the unit are shown 'bombing-up'; a much smaller proportion of AP rounds was stowed in this theatre, where Japanese armour seldom appeared, but some was always carried as it was useful for breaking up the timbers of enemy bunkers. The bulk of the ammunition load consisted of HE shell and flat-ended canister rounds, the latter being used not only as a man-killer but also to clear the line of sight in close country. The Sikh VCO on the right is a Jemadar, and wears the standard RAC pattern 'skeleton order' complete with revolver and ammunition pouch.

E2: *M3A3 of Yugoslav 1st Partisan Tank Brigade, 1944–45*

Following a series of disastrous defeats on the Eastern Front in 1944 the Germans decided to shorten their line by slowly withdrawing from the Balkan Peninsula. In Yugoslavia the strong Partisan Movement, faced now by a less formidable opposition, greatly extended the scope of their operations, and were supplied with heavy weapons by both the Red Army and the Western Allies. A number of these vehicles, in basic Olive Drab with random stripes of Field Brown, were handed over at Bari after a brief instructional course, the crews wearing British battledress and black berets with red star badges. The Communist star also appears in the centre of the national flag, which has been painted on the hull side, and on the sponson plates. The tank's name LOVĆEN is painted on both sides of the turret (starboard presentation inset) and, loosely translated, means 'Little Darling'—perhaps a reference to our crew member, who is shown by photographs to have been one of at least two female partisans serving with the unit. The Brigade (a slightly ambitious term) was shipped across to Dalmatia and took part in several local actions during the last phase of the liberation.

F1: *M5A1 of 1st French Armoured Division; Italy, 1944–45*

The vehicle's overall finish is in Olive Drab, with the following markings on the hull sides (from back to front): tank number '61' in yellow; red, white and blue divisional sign, repeated on the turret roof; and a narrow vertical tricolour. On the top left corner of the glacis plate, as viewed, is a white oblong with coloured bars and an Olive Drab letter 'G'; this type of coding, with various numbers and colours of bars and differing unit code letters, was often seen on US and Allied armour on the 5th Army sector of the Italian front, but precise details of the system remain, for the present, uncertain. On the lower glacis the narrow tricolour symbol has been repeated with a paler shade of blue, while above it is a French service number-plate; to the right is the vehicle's bridge classification circle. The crew are wearing standard US tank helmets over woollen 'beanie' caps, and American M1941 field jackets.

Right: *Brigadier-Chef of 12e Chasseurs d'Afrique French 2e Division Blindée; Paris, August 1944*

Pale blue and yellow sidecap of the Chasseurs d'Afrique; US Olive Drab herringbone twill overall; US web gaiters and US boots. Sleeve rank insignia, one silver over two khaki bars, with regimental insignia in yellow on dark blue below —in fact, the regiment's pre-war collar patch. The Brigadier-Chef is examining two types of 37mm ammunition—solid AP shot with an olive green head and yellow stencils, and incendiary which has a grey head with a purple band.

F2: *75mm Howitzer Motor Carriage M8 of 1er Régiment Etranger de Cavalerie, 5e Division Blindée; North-West Europe, 1944–45*

The 1st Foreign Legion Cavalry was the reconnaissance regiment of this division and was equipped with M8 Greyhound armoured cars, M3A1 White scout cars and, in the support troops, M8 Howitzer Motor Carriages. Note the

th Indian Light Cavalry's M3A1s motor past the scene of a apanese ambush on the road to Mandalay. It was the egimental practice to paint the tank name around the top f the circular mantlet (see Plate E1); this vehicle is Cawnpore'. (Imperial War Museum)

arge hand-painted Allied white star; the ehicle's name, JOFFRE; and the distinctive rench tricolour/number-plates on the hull sides nd glacis. Aft of the vehicle name is one version f the divisional insignia, the same as that of the er Division Blindée but with the addition of the motto FRANCE D'ABORD in the centre; a second ersion, shown inset, also incorporates the egion's green grenade; photographs show both quare and rectangular presentations, depending n the location of the insignia. The white marking on the side of the engine compartment is a tylized letter 'P' (many photographs of the regiment also show 'R') below a sign indicating attalion and squadron. The crew wear US erringbone twill overalls and white-covered egion képis; sergeants and above often wore reen (or green with dark blue top fold) sidecaps ith silver rank diagonals on the left front.

Some M8 Howitzers were also used by the upport company of this division's mechanized nfantry regiment, the Régiment de Marche de la égion Etrangère, carrying the code letter 'C'. In oth cases, the more colourful markings were normally painted over before going into action.

G: *M3A3 Stuart V turret interior, looking forward: and (below) to rear.*
See key on page 25.

H (top): *M3A3 of 501er Régiment de Chars de Combat, French 2e Division Blindée; Paris, August 1944*
The vehicle is finished in overall Olive Drab with the usual French markings. The yellow bar with 'C' below on the hull side is the 501er RCC's tactical symbol within the 2e DB, while the yellow bar-'X' on the glacis indicates attachment to Divisional HQ, possibly as an escort troop. The divisional sign, incorporating a map of France and the Cross of Lorraine, appears only on the port-side sponson plate. The individual tank number '2' and the name D'ORNANO are in blue shadowed with yellow. Crews of this regiment wore US overalls but British black berets, incorporating the pre-war French tank troops' badge of a silver knight's helm over crossed cannons.

H (bottom): *M3A3 Stuart V driver's position, looking forward and right.*
See key on page 25.

39

Notes sur les planches en couleur

A1 Peinture américaine vert olive appliquée partout, barbouillée de boue de couleur pâle pour faire un camouflage; l'étoile jaune et la bande sur la tourelle étaient les insignes nationaux utilisées dans cette campagne; le chiffre '8' est le numéro individuel du char. **A2** Les rayures rouges sur l'étoile indiquent qu'il s'agit du 3ème peloton. Le drapeau national était peint sur tous les véhicules blindés au début des débarquements de la campagne 'Torch', mais plus tard il était normalement effacé à la peinture. 'Rebel' est le nom individuel du char; devant lui, sur le blindage avant de l'encorbellement, on peut voir la marque de la 'C' Company—un disque jaune sur l'extrémité droite d'une barre jaune. **A3** Ce char ne porte aucune marque supplémentaire; celle portée sur la tourelle indique la compagnie et le peloton, celles sur la coque sont des insignes individuels ajoutés par l'équipage.

B1 Ceci est un schéma de camouflage typiquement britannique, utilisé au début de la campagne dans le désert; les signes de reconnaissance rouges et blancs, du style des années 1914–18, sont toujours portés. Le carré jaune sur le côté de la tourelle indique qu'il s'agit de l'escadron 'B'; 'Bellman' est le nom individuel du char, d'après un célèbre chien de chasse. L'insigne de la 7th Armoured Division est peint sur le côté droit du garde-chenille (détail en médaillon). Pendant un certain temps, les soldats de ce régiment ont porté le vieux casque de char américain en cuir marron. Les officiers portaient un calot vert gansé d'or qui était unique en son genre, le 'chapeau de tente'. **B2** Les mêmes couleurs de camouflage, mais ici le vert est peint par dessus les autres tons en tâches appliquées au hasard. Le triangle de l'escadron 'A' et le numéro du 3ème peloton sont peints sur la tourelle; l'insigne de la 7th Armoured Division et le numéro '86' indiquant un régiment au sein d'une division, sont peints sur les garde-chenilles.

C1 Insigne divisionnaire (détail en médaillon) sur le garde-chenille; le numéro 62 sur carré vert indique un régiment au sein de la division—le fond vert indiquant la deuxième brigade dans une division composée de deux brigades. Cercle de l'escadron 'C' peint sur la tourelle. **C2** Le vieux numéro de série américain est à peine visible sous le nom russe. L'étoile rouge sur la tourelle n'était pas normalement peinte sur les chars de construction russe, mais elle était plus courante sur les modèles étrangers dont la silhouette aurait pu être inconnue des tireurs russes.

D1 Les chars individuels de cette unité utilisaient des chiffres au lieu des noms. Le régiment est indiqué par la marque '174'; le 'diabolo' vert-sur-noir est l'insigne de la brigade. Peu de temps après le Jour-J, ce char porte toujours la partie inférieure du système d'échappement conçu pour les voyages en eau profonde, dont il était spécialement équipé pour les débarquements. **D2** L'insigne de la brigade (détail en médaillon) et l'insigne tactique régimentaire '53' sont peints sur la plaque du glacis; la barre blanche sous celui-ci indique que le char est sous la commande directe de l'Armée au lieu de faire partie d'une formation subalterne.

E1 Le filet pare-bombes sur le devant du char obscurcit les deux marques portées sur le blindage avant: code tactique du régiment, le chiffre '37' sur fond jaune et rouge, utilisé par les unités indiennes et l'insigne de la 14th Army. Nom individuel sur le masque du canon: 'Le marteau de Thor'. Marques d'escadron et de peloton sur la tourelle. **E2** Photographié à l'époque où ce char a été livré aux partisans de Tito par les Britanniques à Bari en Italie pendant l'hiver de 1944 à 1945, avec son 'équipière' charmante! Le camouflage est composé de peinture Olive Drab et Field Drab; le drapeau national yougoslave, avec l'étoile des partisans, l'étoile étant répétée sur l'encorbellement; le nom individuel du char est 'Lovćen'.

F1 Insignes divisionnaires sur le côté de la coque et le toit de la tourelle; le numéro individuel du char est '61'; marque du code régimentaire composée de barres de couleur et d'une lettre sur la plaque du glacis (non identifiée). **F2** Différentes versions de l'insigne divisionnaire de la 5eDB étaient peintes sur les véhicules, tantôt carrées, tantôt rectangulaires; le détail (en médaillon) montre une variante qui était souvent utilisée par le 1er REC.

G1 et **G2** Vues d'intérieur de la tourelle du M3A3 Stuart V, face à l'avant (en haut) et à l'arrière. Une légende en langue anglaise se trouve à la page 25.

H1 Le 'C' jaune identifie le 501er RCC: le 'X' indique que ce char tait détaché auprès de l'état-major du Général Leclerc. L'insigne de la division est peint sur l'encorbellement et les nom et numéro individuels du char, '2' et 'D'Ornano', sont peints en bleu et jaune sur le côté de la coque. **H2** Poste du pilote du M3A3, face à l'avant et à la droite; voir la page 25.

Farbtafeln

A1 Panzer in ganz US olivgrün, reichlich beschmiert mit hellem örtlichen Schmutz als Tarnung. Der gelbe Stern und der gelbe Ring um den Turm waren die US-Hoheitszeichen, die in diesem Feldzug benutzt wurden. Die '8' ist die Nummer des individuellen Panzers. **A2** Rote Streifen auf der Stern kennzeichnen den 3. Zug. Die Nationalfahne war auf allen gepanzerten Fahrzeugen anfangs während der 'Torch' Landungen gemalt, wurde jedoch später meistens überstrichen. 'Rebel' ist der Name des individuellen Panzers, davor auf der Vorderplatte der Wannenseite kann man die 'C' Company Markierung sehen—eine gelbe Scheibe über dem rechten Ende eines gelben Streifens. **A3** Keine anderen Markierungen wurden von diesem Panzer getragen; die am Turm zeigt Kompanie und Zug, die am Rumpf sind individuelle Beschriftungen von der Mannschaft hinzugefügt.

B1 Typisches britisches Tarnungsschema anfangs im Wüstenfeldzug; die alten im Stil von 1914–18 rot und weissen Erkennungsstreifen wurden noch getragen. Das gelbe Rechteck an der Turmseite zeigt das 'B' Schwadron an. 'Bellman' ist der Name des individuellen Panzers, nach einem berühmten Jagdhund. Das Zeichen der 7th Armoured Division ist auf den inneren Kettenschutz gemalt (Detailierung ausgesetzt). Dieses Regiment trug für einige Zeit die alten, braunen, ledernen US Army Panzerhelme. Offiziere trugen eine einzigartige 'Schiffchenmütze' von grüner Farbe mit gold verziert, der 'Zelthut'. **B2** Dieselben Tarnfarben, hier jedoch ist das Grün in unregelmässigen Flecken über die anderen Schattierungen aufgetragen. Das Dreieck für 'A' Schwadron und die Nummer für den 3. Zug sind an den Turm gemalt; das Zeichen der 7th Armoured Division und die Nummer '86', das Regiment innerhalb der Division anzeigend, sind auf den Kettenschutz gemalt.

C1 Divisionszeichen am Kettenschutz (Detailierung ausgesetzt); und Nummer 62 auf grünem Rechteck zeigen das Regiment innerhalb der Division an—der grüne Hintergrund zeigt an, dass es die zweite Brigade in einer Zweibrigaden-Division ist. 'C' Schwadronenkreis an den Turm gemalt. **C2** Die alte US Army Seriennummer ist gerade noch sichtbar unter dem russischen Namen. Der rote Stern am Turm war normalerweise nicht auf russisch gebauten Panzern, jedoch öfters an fremden Typenarten, dessen Silhouette den russischen Schützen wohl fremd gewesen sein mag.

D1 Die individuellen Panzer dieser Einheit benutzten Nummern anstelle von Namen. Das Regiment ist erkennbar durch die Markierung '174'; das grün über schwarz 'Diabolo', ist das Brigadezeichen. Kurz nach dem D-Day (Landungstag), trägt dieser Panzer noch den unteren Teil der Auspuff-vorrichtung, der für die Landung montiert wurde und es ihm ermöglichte durch tiefes Wasser zu waten. **D2** Das Brigadezeichen (Detailierung ausgesetzt) und das regimentale taktische Zeichen '53' sind auf der vorderen Rumpfplatte gemalt; der weisse Streifen unter der '53' zeigt an, dass unter direktem Befehl der Armee steht und nicht Teil einer untergeordneten Formation ist.

E1 Der anti-Bomben Maschendraht vorne am Panzer verdeckt die zwei Markierungen, die auf der vorderen Platte getragen wurden: den regi-mentalen taktischen Code '37' auf dem gelben und roten Hintergrund, von indischen Einheiten benutzt, und das Zeichen der 14th Army. Individueller Name auf dem Geschützschild; 'Thor's Hammer'. Schwadronen- und Zugmarkierungen am Turm. **E2** Fotografiert bei der Überreichung an die Partisanen durch die Briten bei Bari, Italien, im Winter 1944-45, komplett mit seinem reizenden 'Mannschaftsmitglied'; Tarnungsfarben in US 'Olive Drab' und 'Field Drab'; jugoslavische Nationalfahne mit dem Partisanenstern und der wiederholten Stern an der Rumpfseitenplatte; individueller Panzername 'Lovćen'.

F1 Divisionszeichen an der Rumpfseite und dem Turmdach; individuelle Panzernummer '61'; Rumpf-Code-Markierung, bestehend aus bunten Streifen und Buchstabe auf der vorderen Rumpfplatte (nicht identifiziert). **F2** Verschiedene Versionen der 5eDB divisionellen Zeichen waren auf die Fahrzeuge gemalt, einige quadratisch, einige rechteckig, die Detailierung (ausgesetzt) zeigt eine Variation oft von den 1er REC benutzt.

G1 und **G2** Innenansicht des M3A3 Stuart V Turmes, vorwärtsschauend (oben) und rückwärts. Eine erklärende Schlüsselung in englisch ist auf Seite 25.

H1 Das gelbe 'C' identifiziert die 501et RCC; das 'X' zeigt an, dass dieser Panzer zu Gen. Leclerc's HQ gehörte. Das Divisions-zeichen ist auf der Rumpfseite, weit vorgesetzt, gemalt, und der individuelle Panzername 'D'Ornano' und die Nummer '2' sind in blau und gelbe auf die Wannenseite gemalt. **H2** Die Position des M3A3 Fahrers, nach vorne und rechts schauend, siehe Seite 25.